6/9/12
Noted spills
on pg. B-1
Ck out: ℞

THE COMPLETE BOOK OF

Natural Cosmetics

by Beatrice Traven

COSMETIC FORMULATIONS BY
Robert L. Goldemberg

ILLUSTRATED BY
Pam Carroll

SIMON AND SCHUSTER
NEW YORK

SBN-671-21769-0
LIBRARY OF CONGRESS CATALOG CARD NUMBER: 74-3247
DESIGNED BY IRVING PERKINS
MANUFACTURED IN THE UNITED STATES OF AMERICA
PRINTED BY THE MURRAY PRINTING COMPANY
BOUND BY AMERICAN BOOK-STRATFORD PRESS, INC.

1   2   3   4   5   6   7   8   9   10

For Lee and Lisa,
whose cheerful patience and cooperation
made this book possible,
and
For Shary, Kathy, and David,
whose love and interest helped make it fun.

Contents

Foreword

T H E whole idea of making cosmetics solely from natural ingredients is an exciting challenge to the professional cosmetic chemist because, for all practical purposes, he simply can't *do* that "commercially" when formulating cosmetics intended for the mass market.

The reasons for this are quite simple, and inescapable. The few 100 percent natural emulsifiers which are available are of limited value. Used alone, lanolin and lecithin (for example) produce heavy-feeling creams reminiscent of the old-fashioned "night creams." Light creams or lotions using either of these as the sole emulsifier are not even possible. And although potent natural preservatives do exist, they bear names like mercury, arsenic, and formaldehyde—great products if you want to embalm a mummy that will last five thousand years, but not exactly recommended for delicate cosmetics to be applied to the living face! The problem seems to be that natural preservatives are often *too* good; they kill all life, not just those bacteria and mold spores which can cause cosmetics to "spoil" after a few weeks unless properly preserved.

So when the subject of making *natural* cosmetics at home first came up, I blanched a bit, sputtered, and then mumbled things like "But that's not possible—there *are* no decent natural emulsifiers which can produce light creams and lotions, no *safe* natural preservatives."

After a while, though, the whole idea began to get to me. Thoughts like "What if . . . ?" began forming. And later, "*But what is natural, anyhow?* How about ordinary soap, for example?

Every time that roast-pig-on-a-spit drips a little fat into that charcoal fire, as a chemist I *know* that a little soap forms down there in those wood ashes." (In fact, that's where lye originally came from, wood ashes, and in backwoods soapmaking it still does.) Our early-American forefathers (or their wives!) made soap at home quite simply: they cooked up pork fat and tallow with wood ashes and water. Would anyone consider it unreasonable, then, if I used soap occasionally as an emulsifier for "natural cosmetics"?

As soon as that question was settled, Dispersible Lecithin (see page 113) resulted, and a full range of creams and lotions became possible.

The other major problem of natural cosmetics, preservation, was met halfway—by using the only truly safe natural preservative, alcohol, where possible. Otherwise these formulas contain no preservative, and most of them must be stored in the refrigerator. Even so, you will find that some of them (those with cucumber juice, for example) won't keep for very long.

It may seem curious that this book can teach you how to make 100 percent natural cosmetics (even though you may have no scientific training at all) while major companies—for all their fancy laboratories, fully automated 1200-gallon tanks and homogenizers—apparently cannot, though it would seem that they'd *like* to, since their ads continually refer to "XYZ natural ingredient." Note however, that not one of these companies offers "100 percent natural" cosmetics, nor are they likely to. Why is that? Why will the only "100 percent natural" cosmetic you ever use probably come from your own kitchen?

It isn't that the large companies don't have the technical know-how, or that they are unwilling to buy fresh natural ingredients to use in their cosmetics. Their problem lies in their very success, in the fact that they must make several hundred thousand jars in order to have a decent supply available for each of their customers (the stores where you go to buy cosmetics).

When you make 200,000 of anything, it takes time—time to make, and time to package. In the case of cosmetics, this may take weeks. Then more weeks go by, during nationwide shipments to thousands of stores, traversing hot deserts in the summertime, or being stalled in unheated freight cars in a snowstorm while crossing the Rockies. That's pretty rough treatment for a delicate emulsion. Then, after the shipment finally arrives, the store clerks may not even unpack the cartons for a while—or perhaps they were instructed to wait until a planned TV ad campaign breaks in their area. Finally, you, the consumer, may not like the product much, and if that happens, tens of thousands of jars of the new cream may just sit around on those store shelves for a year or more, waiting—and sometimes spoiling.

For reasons such as these, commercial cosmetics must be extraordinarily stable. Before marketing, they are subjected to tough "freeze-thaw" tests, and storage tests in special "hot rooms." They must also be essentially sterile when packed, so as not to grow mold, and furthermore they should contain enough *extra* preservative so that you, milady, don't contaminate your jar of cream by dipping into it with fingers which are, well, shall we simply say "not sterilized"?

You just can't produce 100 percent natural cosmetics which meet requirements like that. Natural materials are simply not stable enough, nor can they be well enough preserved to last eighteen months, the minimum usually specified by manufacturers to their own labs for products intended for mass-market sales.

But *you*, making natural cosmetics at home one jar at a time, have no such "distribution headaches." If your product separates, you know perfectly well that all you have to do is give it a few shakes and *presto!*—the emulsion smoothes out and goes together again. And if your jar of cream grows a tiny bit of mold, you'll probably just scrape off the top layer the first time and, if you see that it looks "clean" underneath, keep using it—until more mold grows a week later. At this point you finally toss the jar into the garbage can. But the odds are that you won't write to the "manufacturer" or to Washington about it! You'll simply resolve to make half as much next time, so that you can use it up before it begins to spoil.

Product safety is another area where you have it all over commercial cosmetics. Homemade cosmetics are custom-made, *by* the customer *for* the customer. Are you allergic to strawberries or egg

13

on your face? Well, then, you won't use strawberries or egg in your face cream, will you?

I'd like to touch on one last point before you get on to the book itself: the matter of following recipes exactly. Cosmetic formulas, especially emulsions, are not like food recipes in one respect: their ingredients must be put together in the proper proportions, and they are quite "touchy" in regard to the temperature and speed at which the emulsion is combined. In the factory, cosmetic ingredients are very carefully weighed into large kettles, then heated to definite temperatures and pumped at rather slow and carefully controlled speeds. In the typical American home kitchen, however, it is almost impossible to control these "variables." Most of us have no kitchen scale (although it is a quite common household item in Europe, where even eggs are called for by weight in cookbooks), nor an accurate enough thermometer, nor any way of measuring the proper rate at which emulsions should be put together.

Part of the problem in devising cosmetic formulas for this book, therefore, was to try to make them as foolproof as possible—requiring neither a thermometer nor a scale. Such limitations would appall most professional cosmetic chemists, yet, as you shall see very shortly, we *were* able to do it, and the products themselves are very good indeed. The emulsions (creams and lotions) are elegant and quite light in texture. The solutions and tinctures are not tacky, and the fragrances are natural, strong and believable. All of them can be made with simple kitchen tools by following the indicated procedures carefully.

So relax, stay cool, and have fun as you make your natural cosmetics. And by all means start making your own personal variations on these recipes as soon as you get the hang of it. Just remember to measure out all quantities exactly, and make only careful and *reasonable* substitutions for original ingredients (see the Glossary for ideas). I wish you as much fun as we had.

Robert L. Goldemberg

September 23, 1973

Preface

A T a now legendary (in our family) dinner with friends, the host's lady turned to me and said that she loved our first book, *Here's Egg on Your Face* (never a bad way to begin with an author), but *why* didn't we do a book using all the "wonderful natural ingredients" newly available in supermarkets, drugstores and health food stores.

Between appetizer and soup we explained that *Here's Egg* did indeed glory in the use of many fresh natural ingredients. By the main course we were admitting that, yes, there was a wealth of new material—oils, perfumes, chlorophyll, lecithin, and on and on—that hadn't been readily available to home cosmetic cooks four years ago, when *Here's Egg* was born. And by dessert we could scarcely hold the formulating half of our partnership down.

Since then we've been dedicated and incessant natural-foods shoppers, tracking down ingredients, haunting old herbals and new scientific journals, and cooking up and refining new formulas. The result: *The Complete Book of Natural Cosmetics.*

A WORD ABOUT "NATURAL"

The word "natural" is used very loosely by a variety of people to mean a variety of things. *I* mean a substance that has not been subjected to any process that changes its chemical structure. I mean "as it comes from nature"—but I accept washing, juicing, tincturing or extracting (see EXTRACTS, in the Glossary), grinding, and cooking as within the terms of the definition.

"Natural" is *not* a synonym for either "good" or "healthful." *Plenty of natural substances are poison to you,* inside or out. Lily-of-the-valley pips are natural; but don't eat them! Deadly nightshade is natural, as is the destroying-angel mushroom. And so are poison ivy and poison oak, nettles (very good when cooked, very bad when raw!) and snake venom. So don't fall into the fallacy that assumes that all science is bad, all nature is good. It's simply not true, in life or in cosmetics.

What *is* true is that many natural substances have enormous cosmetic benefits. Some of them have been known for hundreds of years. Some are just coming to light as a result of new scientific studies. And a cosmetic made from natural substances has an enormous edge on a commercial product "based on" the same ingredients. No commercial cosmetic can use raw *whole* natural ingredients, because—as you'll find when you start making your own—they don't keep very well. Like all fresh substances, they should be refrigerated unless the percentage of alcohol (a fine preservative of men and cosmetics) is very high, or unless they contain no water whatsoever. Obviously, a cosmetic made to be shipped at outdoor temperatures, to live on a shelf for perhaps a year and a half, and to live at your house for goodness knows how much longer simply couldn't qualify.

And natural ingredients are *expensive*. Not for you; you'll eat steak dinners on the money you save making your own cosmetics from this book. To manufacturers, though (whose budgets include shipping, labeling, packing, bottling, labor, research, advertising—and, oh, yes, profit), using cheaper synthetic ingredients rather than naturals, and offering fragrance, color and appearance, or perhaps a smidgin of a natural, as a stand-in for a "natural product" is an economic necessity.

But for you, home cosmeticook, the sky is the limit! Nutritionists tell us that whatever goodies a food may contain are at their peak when it is *fresh* and *raw*; vitamins, chlorophyll, minerals, are most readily available when food is fresh. So, whatever cucumber or milk or butter or strawberries or avocado or buttermilk or yogurt or eggs can do for your skin—and there's a considerable amount of evidence that they can do a great deal—they will do best when they're fresh. That's one reason why the cosmetics you'll make from these pages will be special, superior, and different from anything you could buy anywhere, no matter how much money you have to spend.

Another plus in making your own natural cosmetics is that you can tailor-make them for you. Cosmetics you buy are made for the millions; cosmetics you make are your kind, your color, your fragrance, and they suit your needs. We hope that you'll use these recipes as a launching pad to start you off in cosmetic cookery. But like all good recipes, they offer endless variations, limited only by *your* needs and *your* creativity.

A WORD ABOUT SENSITIVITY

For those with sensitive skin or allergies, making their own natural cosmetics has a special added attraction. *Everyone* should test *all* new cosmetics, homemade or otherwise, for possible allergic reactions. A simple and reliable way is this: put a dab of the cosmetic on the sensitive skin inside the crease of your elbow, cover it with an adhesive bandage and leave it covered for twenty-four hours. If, when you take the bandage off, there's no sign of redness or rash, that cosmetic is probably safe for you.

With the recipes in this book, the same precautions should be observed. But when you're in charge of making your own cosmetics, you *know* what goes into each one; you know what you can substitute, and there's no reason ever to end up with a jar of lovely cream that simply doesn't get along with your skin. If you *know* that you're sensitive to strawberries or eggs, for example, just leave them out and substitute ingredients that suit you better.

Naturally, if you use any beauty product that leaves you

itchy, irritated or uncomfortable, you'll discontinue its use. And naturally *no* cosmetic is a substitute for medicine, or should be used when skin is especially sensitive, after a bad sunburn or windburn, or on open sores or cuts. But with reasonable precautions, these recipes should serve you well, and make you feel—and look and smell (even taste!)—better than you ever have before.

So cook away!

Equipment: *What You Need and What You Don't*

I f you do any cooking at all in your kitchen, you probably already have everything you need to start on the recipes in this book. You might, however, want to buy a few extras which will make life easier. But be assured that you can use your regular pots, pans and silver without any worries about "poison" ingredients or chemicals that won't wash off. Everything will wash off with soap and water, and, though you wouldn't want to quaff isopropyl rubbing alcohol, nothing you use will be more mysterious, fearsome or unpalatable than that household standby.

You *can* make almost all of the recipes satisfactorily with a hand-operated egg beater, but you'd be much better off with a portable electric mixer, the kind with at least three speeds (low, medium, high) and with two beaters which eject separately. For these recipes, I *take out one beater* and beat with the other. This way I can get into small jars and beat small batches neatly, without splashing my precious creams around. So when, in the recipes, I refer to electric beating, this is what I mean: *one beater only*.

You will need some small pots and pans. I bought enamel ones in the five-and-ten—a couple of very small ones, a two-cup and another about a quart. These have lasted through many batches, and will surely last through many more. I bought enamel because it's inexpensive and won't react with any of the ingredients in the recipes as aluminum or some other metals might. But, if you like, use Pyrex glass or ceramic pots, or even Pyrex measuring cups (be careful of the handles, though, when the cups are hot!); as long as they can take direct heat, they work just as well.

Many of the recipes call for heating over water. If you have a double boiler, that will work fine. So will a sturdy, heavy baking pan (one that can take direct heat on top of the stove) with two inches or so of water in it. My own favorite is a large electric frying pan that can be half filled with water, turned on, and controlled by twisting the dial. This way, you can put two small pots or Pyrex cups into the water at once and keep them at the same temperature—very important when making emulsions. A friend has used an electric deep-fat fryer with a couple of inches of water in it, and swears by it. Use what you have—though the money you save making cosmetics could easily treat you to an electric helper if you don't already own one.

You'll also need metal measuring spoons—not plastic, which melts gooily at the first sign of real heat—and a few spatulas or wide knives for mixing and smoothing. The best kind, I find, are the inexpensive palette knives you can buy in art-supply stores, about four or five inches long, flexible, with a stainless-steel blade.

You'll also want a narrow rubber scraper, maybe two of different sizes for getting the last bit of goody out of the pan; a few eye droppers for measuring tiny amounts of things like food colors and perfumes; a couple of plastic or Pyrex measuring cups; and perhaps a pair of strong metal forceps for handling hot jars. And *that's all.*

Of course you'll need jars and bottles, and I strongly suggest that you start pestering everybody now for heavy, tight-closing glass jars and bottles of various sizes, plus pretty ones (also tight-closing) for doing gifts up in style. Never *give* a full bottle unless you get two empties back! That way you'll train your friends right and never be stuck with a panful of cream and nothing but a teacup to pour it into. (It's happened to me!) Save all the useful cosmetic jars and bottles you buy (although you'll be buying less now and enjoying it much, much more). Save baby-food jars (invaluable), peanut-butter jars, jelly jars, everything. But stay away from plastic if you can; often it's not boilable, and some plastics react to some of the ingredients, or tend to "leak" oil or fragrance.

Wash each container carefully to get rid of all the old odors, and make sure it's absolutely dry before you put it away. I always throw away the insides of the covers, if there are any; they seem to be a great place for mold to start. Use aluminum foil instead.

You might also like to invest in some inexpensive decorative labels. But homemade ones—paper, or freezer tape, or write-on paper mending tape—are perfectly fine. You should *label everything you make* with its name. After a while, no matter how good your memory is, the cream for one part of you begins to look like the mask for another. All the perishable cosmetics should be labeled as well with the *date* you made them. And any special instructions should be on the label, too. Remember that most of these cosmetics will end up in your refrigerator, and all of them look luscious and smell luscious. Don't take the chance of an eager child or grownup taking a swig of something that's meant only for the *outside* of you. In our house we label BIG AND BRIGHT. I also recommend a special plastic "crisper" kind of closed box on one shelf that's *only for cosmetics.* That way you won't end up "moisturizing" the inside of your tummy.

Another "extra" that you might want, and that I strongly recommend, is a notebook labeled "Natural Cosmetics," in which you keep track of all your products, just the way professional cosmetic chemists do. The more information you cram into this book, about ingredients, batches, failures (if you have them), variations, "shelf life" times, and observations, the more you'll learn and grow.

I cannot think of another thing. If you have all of the above, which you can buy for less than the price of a really "luxurious" eye cream, you are in business—the natural-cosmetic business— and for pleasure!

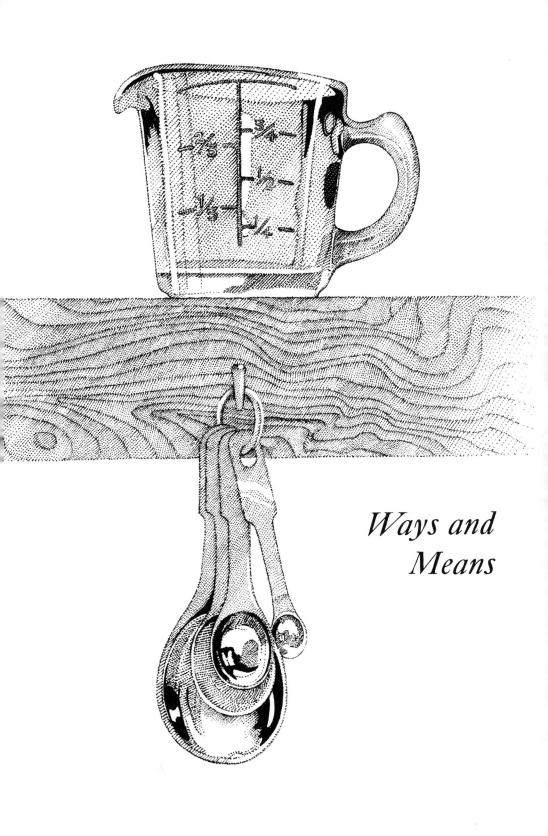

Ways and Means

T H E S E recipes are actually the result of two separate processes. First they were painstakingly formulated by a master cosmetic chemist in his lab, set down in scientific terms, weighed in grams and ounces, aged and tested, just the way the cosmetics you buy (which he's also had many years of experience formulating) are created.

Then his formulas, notes, and products were taken into the kitchen and translated into the language *I* know—teaspoons and tablespoons and measuring cups—and I *re*made them, making sure that my results turned out as beautifully as his before I passed them and said, "Yes, they're ready for the book."

Since the master formulator and the kitchen tester happen to be husband and wife, you can imagine how many lively discussions there have been over coffee or moisture cream and sometimes even over the telephone (from lab extension to kitchen extension), before two picky perfectionists (one brandishing his lab stirrer, the other her trusty one-beater hand mixer) agreed on every single recipe given here.

In the years that we've been making cosmetics at home (and writing books about them), we've both mellowed a little and learned a lot about how to translate lab techniques to the kitchen. No longer do we end up nose to nose over whether to describe a recipe (as you would a formula) in terms of weight measurements. On the other hand, no longer do *I* question the need for precise measurements in the recipes instead of "a pinch" of this or "a bit" of that. "Teaspoon" means level teaspoonful; "cup" means measuring cup; "simmer" means that slow lazy rising of small bubbles to the surface of a brew *before* it is hot enough to come to a rolling boil. Similarly, I've tried not to say "whip" (to beat in air) when I mean "mix" (merely agitating together until the mixture is homogenous). Sometimes these terms are elusive. "Warm," "hot," "cool," "room temperature," "stiff," "thin," "heavy," "smooth" are descriptive words which allow for individual interpretation, though "everybody knows" what they mean in general. We've tried not to let the success of a recipe hang on the interpretation of such words. In fact, most of the recipes are so skillfully formulated that if they go wrong for any reason, you can back up, correct whatever went wrong, and try again with the same batch until you get it right.

I think that if you're really a serious cosmeticook, the best way to use this book is to *read it from cover to cover* (as I do a cookbook) for ideas, techniques, and a general familiarity with the ingredients and how they're combined. Then, when you've picked out the recipes you want to work on, *read each one through thoroughly before you begin*. Read up on all the ingredients in the Glossary and learn more about their properties and their history (which makes using them more fun), and perhaps get some idea of how to make ingredient substitutions when the time comes for your own experiments.

Though you *can* be creative with ingredients, you'd better stay close to text on procedures. In general, an emulsion must be made by combining the two phases (oily and watery materials) together at the *same temperature*, slowly, then cooling the mixture gradually, continually stirring as you do so. If they are of unequal temperatures when you mix them together, or if you jar them while they're too hot, or if you get lazy and think you can get away without stirring so much, beware! You'll get *something*, but it won't be the lovely smooth emulsion you're after. It may curdle, or separate quickly. Sometimes you can rewarm and start over. But not always. So trust the directions; they're as easy as I could make them and still get the proper results. If you simplify them further, or try to take shortcuts, you may end up with a hopeless mess of goo and have to start all over from the beginning.

Sometimes an emergency may call you away from your pots and pans, and when you get back your mix has thickened up or evaporated off too much water. If this happens, try working in an additional tablespoon or so of warm water, to make up for what was lost. Do this a little at a time and "baby" it in; if you can do it successfully, you'll be more than rewarded by a "saved" cream or lotion.

Be careful of the jars and bottles you use to store your treasured finished products. Make sure they are scrupulously *clean* and *dry* before you use them; a bit of extra water in the bottom may contain just the "bugs" (bacteria) that cause your cream to spoil. Always use jars that are boilable, so that heat won't crack or buckle them. I like glass, but some plastic containers are also O.K. to use. If cosmetic creams came in them, plastic jars and bottles are probably safe for your products. But some plastics react to oils or perfumes and let them "leak" through the wall of the jar. *Don't* use untinned copper, brass, silver or other metal containers that might react with any of the ingredients and tarnish or rust, thereby spoiling your handiwork.

Try, too, to *fill your jars to the brim* if you can; avoid air bubbles when you load thick or stiff mixtures. As with food, the more contact you allow with air, the quicker the product will go bad. So full jars, without air bubbles, last longer than half-empty ones.

Even though your jars and bottles are boilable, don't trust them too far. A cold jar placed in hot water is apt to crack, no matter how "boilable" it is. So always start with the jars at room temperature, or, if you're going to pour something hot or cold into them, have the jars at more or less the temperature of the mix. If you have to heat or cool them in the course of a recipe, do so gently and slowly. Otherwise, maybe, *Crrrrunch!*, *Splat!* and "#%%%!!**!"

You'll notice that in nearly all the recipes we ask that mixtures be heated over hot water. That's because fats and oils burn if you give them the slightest opportunity; Soap Soup might bubble over gooily onto your stovetop; alcohol can evaporate. So always do your heating in a wide, low pan (like an electric fry pan or a baking pan) or in a double boiler. Never underestimate the importance of *gentle* heating and *slow* cooling. Sometimes, if you're very adept, you can get away with cooling a jar of cream in a bowl of ice water, *beating all the while* and continually scraping down the sides, so that the whole amount cools at the same rate. But this is tricky and takes a little technique. It's worth learning, though, especially if you're the kind who gets tired of beating and beating and beating and wants to stop before the cooling is completed.

Finally, the easiest way to get gloppy creams and lotions off your kitchenware is to wipe it off first (with paper toweling), rinse with very hot running water, and then wash with soap and water. If the glop is fatty, use a little ammonia, which "cuts" fat. If it's waxy, warm the utensil, to flow off some of the wax and make the remainder a thinner layer, therefore easier to remove; or, conversely, chill or freeze it, and the wax can sometimes be cracked right off. None of the ingredients used here should be really hard to get off, or should damage your pots or silverware in any way. An amazing number of them are edible (see the Glossary). But some are not, and so, as everybody's mother used to say, "When in doubt, do without." Or, translated into kitchen talk: Don't eat it unless you've met it—*and et it*—before!

Fine and Picky Points to Ponder

W H A T makes a cosmetic a cosmetic, anyway? The history of beauty is intimately linked with what in ancient times passed as "medicine." The same herbs, potions, poultices and brews that were optimistically offered as cures for the body also were treated as beautifiers for the face. Nicholas Culpeper (*Complete Herbal*) in the middle of the seventeenth century assured his readers not only that cucumbers were "excellent good for a hot stomach and hot liver," but that "the face being washed with their juice cleanseth the skin, and is excellent good for hot rheums in the eyes." And, if that were not enough, "the seed is excellent good to provoke urine [and] there is not a better remedy growing for ulcers in the bladder. . . . The face being washed with the same [cucumber] water cureth the reddest face that is; it is also excellent good for sunburning, freckles and morphew." Quite a list of virtues in one single green *Cucumis sativus*!

Today, though, we are scrupulous about defining as a drug any product that makes curative claims. Well, then, what is a cosmetic? Does it *do* anything? How can you recognize a good one, a great one, from one that is a poor thing with no virtues at all?

When I was still only a consumer, before I had met and married (is he looking over my shoulder?) one of the finest and most original cosmetic formulators in the profession, I'd bring home each new jar and bottle with emotions that wavered between ecstatic hope and despondent doubt. Each new purchase was going to do "everything," but two weeks later it was a "failure" and had done "nothing."

Now that I've been privileged to learn something of the inner workings of the "mysteries," I know that there are no mysteries at all—and no need for disillusionments, either. A good cosmetic does do what it is made to do, and that can be defined. It does not do magic, but it does do good. It conditions or moisturizes, oils, cools, astringes, stimulates, soothes, cleanses, tones, restores normal acidity, deodorizes or glosses, and that's by no means all! And if it's good, it does its job well and gives aesthetic and sensuous pleasure.

With that as a starting point, let's look at some of the many varieties of cosmetics that are on the market, in this book, and probably on your shelves, and see what they are and what they're supposed to be.

Let's start with a major family group, *alcoholic solutions*; that includes perfumes, colognes, toilet waters, aftershaves, astringents, and the like. All these products are fairly simple solutions of perfume oil in alcohol and water, with perhaps some "conditioners" added.

Perfume is the "top of the line." It contains the highest percentage of both perfume oil (10 to 25 percent) and alcohol, plus, usually, a bit of water (5 to 10 percent) to "round off" the fragrance. Toilet waters come next; traditionally they're between the expensive perfumes and the fairly inexpensive colognes. Toilet waters contain 5 to 10 percent perfume, about 10 to 15 percent water, and the remainder (75 to 85 percent) alcohol. Colognes have only 2 to 5 percent perfume, as much water as the perfume oil will tolerate without going cloudy (usually 20 to 30 percent), and the rest alcohol. As for aftershaves, they're similar to colognes, but have even less perfume (usually 1 to 3 percent), and 30 to 65 percent alcohol (depending on the zing required). The rest of the aftershave is water, plus moisturizers and healing ingredients to make those shaving scrapes and nicks feel better.

So when *you* make these products, aim for a pleasing mixture of perfume and color, a good "skin feel" that doesn't leave any "tackiness" afterward, a sparkling clear, very personal product that does what it's designed to do, and does it with style.

Another large cosmetic family are the *water solutions*. These include shampoos and liquid bubble baths (usually about 60 percent water, 20 to 30 percent detergent, and the rest foam stabilizers and thickeners). Skin fresheners too are mostly water with a little alcohol, fragrance and moisturizers of some kind. (There was even a memorable product on the market a while back that was 100 percent water in a spray can, and another that was water plus one drop of perfume and two drops of dye. *That's* carrying water solutions a bit too far!)

A good shampoo should give you plenty of rich lather and conditioning but not too much cleaning power (or you'll complain of flyaway hair). A bubble bath pleases if it foams readily, smells good, and perhaps helps soften the water so that the ring around the bathtub that plagues bathers in hard-water areas isn't so noticeable. As for skin fresheners, their main job is to cool and refresh as they remove the last bit of greasy residue after cream-cleaning. Sometimes a bit of astringent is used in them, and they usually smell good and look good—lightly colored and sparkling clear.

The biggest and most important of the cosmetic families are *emulsions*. Without emulsions, there'd be no creams and lotions, and since sophisticated cosmetic houses offer a cream and lotion for nearly every part of you, it's hard to imagine a cosmetic shelf without them.

Basically there are two kinds of emulsions: oil-in-water (O/W), in which oil droplets are dispersed in water (like milk), and water-in-oil (W/O), in which the water droplets are dispersed, or wrapped up in, oil (like mayonnaise). Since the product takes its personality from the "enrobing" substance, O/W emulsions are nongreasy, cool and "vanishing," and W/O are rich, emollient and "nourishing." To test whether an emulsion is W/O or O/W, spread a thin film of your product on a shiny knife blade, add a drop or so of water, and try to work it in. If the water goes in readily, you have an O/W product. If it beads and refuses to mix, it's W/O.

Usually creams also contain some kind of wax or waxy material to help stiffen them, plus various other goodies: moisturizers, perfume, color, and other special "actives": vitamins, perhaps, or protein, or some super skin enrichers, plus emulsifiers (substances which help the emulsion to form) and stabilizers (to keep it together).

The aesthetics of making elegant creams and lotions take up much of a cosmetic formulator's time and attention. The products should be smooth and of the right stiffness (eye creams soft, so that you don't have to stretch under-eye tissue to pat them on, throat sticks stiff, so that you massage as you apply, and so on). Lotions should be rich but not sticky, thin if they have to spread a long way (like suntans or body lotions), slightly thicker if they ought to stay where they're put (like "intensive-care" hand creams).

If you want to judge your product the way the pros do, first take a dab of it on a small spatula, look at it, smell it, and feel its consistency. Then rub a bit on the back of your hand, using the sensitive ball of your index finger to really "experience" it. Is it greasy? Does it have the right amount of "slip" for the job? Does it feel tacky or sticky? What is its "initial feel," its "middle feel," its "end feel"? When you open the jar, does it look and smell appealing? Does it seem to go into your skin quickly, or does it just lie there? Does it "cut" well? (To test this, dip your finger in and out; does a *long* "peak" pull out after your finger, or a *short* one? The cosmetic chemist is concerned about this "length of the cut." If it's too stringy, something is wrong with the emulsion; perhaps it wasn't mixed enough during the cooling process.)

In testing your own creams, try to evaluate them honestly, and if they don't measure up, experiment! Make adjustments in the process or recipe. If you want your cream or lotion to feel richer or slipperier, a bit of mineral oil might help, or some paraffin wax. (If your recipe calls for three tablespoons of some oil or oily mixture, try using only two, and replace the third with the mineral oil or paraffin.) Is your product too rich, too heavy? Switch part of your heavy oil to a lighter oil, like apricot kernel. Read the Glossary carefully and try a few substitutes so that you can get *your* cream just right for *you*. That's the fun—and the art—of cosmetic cookery!

Some of the easiest products to make, and some of the most rewarding, are the *emollient oils*—suntans, body oils, makeup removers, bath oils, hair sheens, brilliantines, and the like. These are simply mixtures of oils, skillfully blended to spread easily and evenly and to carry their special "active" goodies to the skin and the hair. They look clear and beautiful, and smell divine. They should provide maximum emolliency with minimum feel of "grease."

The prima donnas of cosmetics are the *clear gels*. Sometimes you can make them just by adding the right gum to water- or alcohol-based solutions. If the gum isn't too sticky, dissolves completely and sets up just right, hooray!—you've got a product. But that's the exception; usually all the other ingredients combined gang up on the gum, and the magical gelling just doesn't happen.

Many commercial clear gels contain no gum at all. They are "microemulsion systems"—actually thick emulsions but with particles so tiny that they're invisible to the naked eye (transparent).

This particular kind of system is very unstable, and it's a real trick to achieve and keep through "thick and thin" (like freezing and thawing!). The clear gels you will be making from these pages have been carefully worked out to gel and stay gelled, but again that's the formulator's art. If you experiment too much with their innards, you might just find yourself with an *un*-gel, or an unclear clear gel; either way, it will give you a much more humble appreciation of the "just right" sparkling *stiff* clear gel that stays where it's put, is absolutely transparent and nonsticky, and rinses off with pure, clear water.

The "big gun" of the *stick products* is lipstick—a mixture of oils and waxes melted together, with dyes (soluble colors) added to stain the lips for long-lasting effect, and pigments (insoluble colors) included to give covering power and to help smooth over tiny skin and lip imperfections. The pigments are usually ground in part of the oil before the stick is made, to ensure the smooth color. The dyes are added later in the process.

Other sticks, like throat sticks, for instance, are made more or less the same way, with waxes and oils, but without the color. Deodorant sticks and cologne sticks are different; they're formed by dissolving soap in alcohol to make a stiff gel (the stick base) and then lacing the mix with "active" ingredients. Blusher sticks are made this way, too, with a bit of pink or red dye added for the "blush."

When you make stick cosmetics, you'll judge their success by the smooth texture of the stick, its stiffness, and how well the "actives" do the job. Oh, and how well did you do yours—loading it into the holder so that there are no air bubbles or empty spaces? You want a stick with a bit of "drag" but no stickiness afterward, sometimes, as in throat stick, melting on contact with the surface, other times, perhaps, keeping its stiffness to the end.

Another category of cosmetics, *aerosols*, is really outside the reach of home cosmeticooks, simply because you don't have the equipment to load the containers with aerosol gas. Commercially, the procedure is complex. The gas, loaded into the can under pressure, actually becomes a liquid which mixes intimately into the product), and when the button on the can is pushed to release the pressure, gas and product come out together. Finally the gas "bursts out" to form a fine spray (as in deodorants), a rich foam (shaving creams), or even a fine dry powder.

Powder products are almost always based on talc these days, an earth product dug out of the ground and washed carefully to remove any alkaline or acid materials. Talc is the softest of all minerals, and its texture is perfect for skin products, unctuous and slippery because of its "platelet" crystal structure (the flat crystals just slide right over each other as you rub it on). Sometimes, as in after-bath powder or foot powder, various other absorbent or "active" ingredients are added, or a bit of emollient (like lanolin or mineral oil) is worked in to prevent the powder from drying out your skin. The powders *you* make should be smooth, perfectly free of lumps, wonderful-smelling, and good to look at. They should do a job of drying up that last bit of after-bath moisture without drying up *you*, and be effective at whatever other job you give them to do, from deodorizing to soothing baby's bottom.

And now, out with the pots and pans; it's time to do battle with "sunburning, freckles and morphew."

*Fruit and
Vegetable
Cosmetics*

T H E R E seems to be something basic in our makeup (no pun intended) that makes us yearn to squeeze or slather or pat on our outsides the things that feel good on our insides. And the impulse isn't all that illogical. We need moisture inside and out, oils inside and out, acids, proteins, vitamins inside and out, to keep us at our best. Why, then, shouldn't we find the *sources* of our inside and our outside well-being in the same substances?

In fact, the oldest cosmetic formularies we know offer advice on the virtues of fruits and vegetables—lemon, strawberry, cucumber, garlic, lettuce—in enhancing and preserving beauty. Modern cosmetics often use these fragrances (all right, *not* garlic!) and colors to suggest natural ingredients, but *you* can make your own fresh, wholesome cosmetics using the real thing.

For a really cool, lovely and *easy* opener, try

Grapefruit Bracer

> 2 tablespoons fresh strained (or canned, *without sugar*)
> grapefruit juice
> ½ to 1 teaspoon peppermint extract
> 2 drops green food color
> ¾ cup 70 percent ethanol alcohol

Combine all ingredients in an 8-ounce jar, screw the top on, shake, and *voilà!*—a beautiful summertime astringent.

If you use fresh grapefruit juice, try adding a bit of very finely grated rind for its perfume. And do experiment with the amount of peppermint extract; some hearts (and eyes) are sturdier than others.

If you're really rugged, or if your man is, try substituting a bit of ordinary 70 percent rubbing alcohol (isopropyl) for part of the ethanol; perhaps ¼ cup isopropyl and ½ cup ethanol alcohols. This is an especially rugged pick-me-up for oily, large-pore skins.

Grapefruit Bracer will keep a long time without refrigeration because of the high alcohol content, but it's especially zingy when it's chilled, so you may want to refrigerate anyway. Try using lemon or tangerine juice as a grapefruit substitute, varying food coloring to match. Lovely as an aftershave too.

LABEL: *Keep away from eye area.*

Apple Cheeks Toning Lotion

½ cup apple juice (fresh strained, or bottled)
¼ cup 70 percent isopropyl alcohol
¼ cup witch hazel

Shake these together and prepare to be surprised! A sparkling appley lotion results, which tingles when you apply it, stimulates circulation, smells of alcohol when you first put it on, but then of delicious apple.

The pectin in the apple juice is soothing and enriching to skin, the alcohol slightly drying, the witch hazel astringent, so this is an especially appealing lotion for teen-age skin. And the silky feel it leaves is really lovely. Try it as a "smoother" and "tightener" before you apply makeup base.

Apple Cheeks doesn't need to be kept in the refrigerator, as the alcohol will help keep it indefinitely, but in hot weather you might like it that way.

LABEL: *Keep away from eye area.*

Lime Tonic

½ whole lime, rind and all
½ cup witch hazel
¼ cup 70 percent ethanol alcohol
½ teaspoon corn syrup
1 egg white

Put all ingredients in your blender and blend at high speed until you have a smooth liquid. If your blender is not too efficient, or if you want a really elegant product, give it a "polish filter":

Cut a circle out of good-quality paper toweling (the kind that won't disintegrate when it gets wet), fold it in half, then in half again, so that it looks like an ice-cream cone. Then, holding two thicknesses together, open it out so that it forms a cornucopia. Put it into the mouth of your jar, and carefully pour your liquid through.

This is a lovely conditioner for oily skin, and especially nice as an aftershave for lime-loving men. The lime is acid and astringent, the corn syrup is a fine humectant (holds moisture to the skin), the egg white adds silkiness and tightening, and the witch hazel is soothing and astringent. You won't want perfume or food coloring for this one; the exotic fragrance of the lime rind is really in a class by itself.

LABEL: *Keep away from eye area.*

Creamy Fruit Frappé Lotion

With Creamy Fruit Frappé Lotion (if you can say it, you can make it!) you'll be making an emulsion, which means you'll really cut your eye teeth as a cosmeticook *and* learn a few things about customizing cosmetics. *I* call this ABC Lotion, because I like to make it with *A*pple, *B*anana and *C*ucumber. But once you've mastered the principle, you can make endless substitutions, depending on what *you* like and what best suits your skin.

This principle of a basic, or "mother," recipe plus a variable portion makes it possible for you to make and store large quantities of the "mother" in advance and then, when you're ready, add the fresh, more perishable ingredients of the variable portion, or make several personalized variations of the same recipe. So here goes: Creamy Fruit Frappé Lotion, a "mother" and an ABC variable.

PHASE A (THE "MOTHER"):
- 1 whole egg
- ¼ cup apricot-kernel (persic) oil
- ½ cup plain yogurt
- 2 tablespoons Dispersible Lecithin (see recipe, page 113)

43

PHASE B (ABC VARIABLE—THE "BABY"):

> 2 tablespoons whole apple juice (whole unpeeled apple, grated or ground or run through electric juicer)
> 2 tablespoons banana and tapioca strained baby food
> 2 tablespoons whole cucumber juice (whole cuke with skin, grated or ground or run through electric juicer)
> 2 teaspoons fresh strained (or reconstituted) lemon juice

PLUS:

> 4 tablespoons witch hazel
> 3 heaping tablespoons Slippery-Elm Gelée (see recipe, page 106)

Beat Phase A together with your electric beater until thoroughly smooth. Then set it aside or, if you're not going to do the rest of the recipe right away, store it in the refrigerator; it will keep several weeks. This is your "mother."

Then beat together in the same way, until smooth, the ABC-variable portion of Phase B: apple, banana tapioca and cucumber (or your own substitutions, which I'll talk about in a minute). When this is done, slowly add the witch hazel, and finally the Slippery-Elm Gelée, beating all the while to keep the mixture smooth.

Now you have two separate phases, "mother" (A) and "child" (B). Simply add B to A, pouring in a slow, steady stream as you beat, and you have created something wonderful.

You now have a cup and a half of the most luxurious, skin-loving lotion you've ever met, with a "pH" (acidity or alkalinity level—in this case, acidity) in the normal-skin range—about 5.5. It's a pale-green emulsion, rich in feel, with the skin-loving qualities of cucumber and apple pectin, the protein content of egg and yogurt, the astringency of witch hazel, and the emolliency of apricot-kernel oil. Add to all these the "natural skin oil" qualities of lecithin, and you've really got an extraordinary winner.

Try it when your skin is itchy and dry from too much winter cold or central heating. Or use it as a rich "intensive-care"-type hand lotion. Best of all, give it to your mother-in-law or any senior citizen you know as an antidote for the dry, scaly skin most older people have to cope with. I promise you, you'll never have enough on hand to meet the demand!

As for substitutions, I've tried and liked carrot juice (lots of vitamin A) in place of the cucumber, fresh strained tomato for the apple (slightly more acid), and mashed avocado (lovely, oil-rich and unctuous) for the banana tapioca, in about the same amounts. Be creative, pore through the Glossary for likely substitutes, and decide on the variations *you* like best.

As for the keeping qualities, no mixture containing water as an ingredient (and that includes the water component of vegetables and fruits) keeps long without refrigeration. I've kept this lotion for several months refrigerated, and you may do better. But remember that it's the *freshness* that gives natural cosmetics a special quality, so be prepared to make them in small amounts and make them often. The virtue of the "mother" system is that you can make a larger quantity of "mother" and then vary your finished products, or you can keep "mother" safely tucked away in the refrig until the day you happen to have some time to spare, as well as some bits of apple, banana tapioca and cucumber (or your variation choices). But a note of caution: do let "mother" warm to room temperature while you're stirring up the "baby," so that when you combine them their temperatures will be about the same.

Hot Fruit Cap Hair Treatment

      6 tablespoons Lecithin Base (see recipe, page 114)

      3 tablespoons fresh strained (or reconstituted) lemon juice

      2 drops balsam scent (available at candle supply stores)

The easiest way to make Hot Fruit Cap is in a heavy wide-mouthed glass jar that holds about a cup. That way you can mix, warm, stir, and store all in the same container and not end up with four dirty dishes to wash. Make sure the jar you use can take boiling, though. The best ones are those that come with commercial canned vegetables or fruits *cooked inside.*

Measure your Lecithin Base into this jar *first,* by preheating a tablespoon and dipping the thick stuff out, then squeegeeing it clean with your finger. Set the jar over hot water. (I like using an electric frying pan full of water for this; it's easy to handle, can be easily regulated, and doesn't tip over! But you can use any wide low pan on the stove *with flame kept low*, or an electric deep-fry, or even a double boiler.) Heat the Lecithin Base until it melts, then remove from heat and stir in the lemon juice slowly, using your electric beater. Keep stirring slowly and faithfully until the mixture cools to room temperature. Add the balsam fragrance.

Don't worry if, as you stir and cool, your beautiful golden emulsion seems to crack and leak and a bit of liquid (lemon juice or water) "breaks out." This is apt to happen if you've overshot the lemon juice or added it too quickly. If it does, just add another tablespoon or so of Lecithin Base, reheat a bit if necessary, restir, and everything will be fine.

If your hair is dry or frazzled, sun-damaged or bleach-damaged, split-ended or whatever, this treatment is for you. Rub it in thoroughly, put on your electric hot cap (or ask your beauty parlor to let you use theirs) and let Hot Fruit Cap work for about five minutes. If you don't have an electric hot cap *or* a beauty parlor, use hot towels over a plastic shower cap, but the results won't be as dramatic.

When you're done, rinse the treatment out with water, leaving a bit in the hair; or, if you can't stand it, shampoo *lightly*. You really want some of that goodness left on your hair. It will amaze you!

Lemon Cream

PHASE A (THE "MOTHER"):
   4 tablespoons lanolin
   2 tablespoons solid vegetable shortening
   3 tablespoons peanut oil

PHASE B (THE VARIABLE):

- 2 tablespoons corn syrup
- ¼ cup plus 1 tablespoon fresh strained (or reconstituted) lemon juice
- ½ teaspoon lemon extract (or, if you're really gung-ho, tincture of fresh lemon rind)

PHASE C:

- 3 tablespoons water (measure precisely!)

This is a more complex emulsion, but practically foolproof, and it too can be made in one jar (if you hate washing dishes as much as I do!). You'll need a wide-mouthed boilable jar of 12 ounces or so.

First combine Phase A ingredients by melting them over hot water till the jar can just barely be touched with your hand. This is the "mother," which you can keep indefinitely, unrefrigerated, for as long as you want to.

Now mix together Phase B (which should be at room temperature). Add B to A *slowly, stirring by hand* until A has taken up all of B. Then cap the jar and *shake hard*. Keep shaking. As the contents cool, a lovely smooth lotion will form. (If you want to speed things up a bit, hold the jar under cold running water now and then as you shake.)

Be sure your lotion is at room temperature before taking the final step; if you can't be patient at this stage, let it sit and come back to it later, or even the next day. Now, finally, add the 3 tablespoons of water to the contents of the jar, *one tablespoon at a time*, whipping with the highest speed of your electric beater. If you do this right, you'll get a gorgeous, rich, thick *cream*. But if you don't, and a bit of water separates out, don't despair. Carefully pour off a few drops and beat the rest in again. *Voilà!*—Lemon Cream.

Lemon juice has been touted as a skin purifier and whitener as far back as cosmetic formularies go. In this recipe it creates an acid pH (see the Glossary) and helps neutralize the drying alkaline effects of many soaps and cosmetics on the skin. Lanolin is the sheep's equivalent of human sebum, the waxy fat that our skin exudes. It's also one of the best humectants known, holding water

47

to the skin, hence "moisturizing." Peanut oil is light and lubricating. Corn syrup, a natural sugar, is used here for its moisturizing qualities, too. And lemon extract—well, it's perfume, and used just for pleasure!

You can make the "mother" for this cream in larger amounts, store it, and then whip up batches of fresh cream when the spirit moves you. Or, even more fun, make variation batches—Strawberry Cream (substituting strawberry juice for lemon, strawberry extract for lemon extract), Peach Cream, Apple Cream, Parsley Cream, Lettuce Cream, or what you will. Just make sure your fruit or vegetable ingredients are fresh and strained. These creams keep well, but I always refrigerate mine. They never seem to last long enough to go bad!

Pineapple-Papaya Paw Cream

This is something special: a hand cream guaranteed to make rough, scaly, dried-out old hands look like new. The secret is in the pineapple and papaya juices; both contain a natural enzyme used to tenderize meat (you've probably sprinkled it over many a tough chuck steak in your kitchen under various commercial names), and they help do the same job for you. This cream softens and smooths beautifully. So if you tend to hide your hands under the table when someone says you're pretty, try Pineapple-Papaya Paw.

PHASE A:

    3 tablespoons stearic acid, flaked (available at candle supply stores)

    2 tablespoons sweet almond oil (or apricot-kernel, sesame, sunflower, mink—any light, penetrating oil)

    1 teaspoon liquid lecithin

    2 tablespoons glycerine

PHASE B:

½ cup Soap Soup solution (see recipe, page 112)
¼ cup fresh strained (or frozen, unsweetened) pineapple juice
¼ cup fresh strained (or canned, unsweetened) papaya juice
1 drop green food coloring
3 drops yellow food coloring

First make your Soap Soup by shaving one ounce of pure soap into a cup of water and boiling them together until the soap dissolves. An easy way to do this (if you're not making large quantities, as described on page 112) is to take a small bar of any white soft soap which is 99 and 44/100 percent pure and floats, and either divide the bar so that you get a one-ounce chunk *or use one cup of water to each ounce* shown on the label of the bar. Shave it up by hand or in your blender, then boil the water and the soap together to get a Soap Soup which will last indefinitely and can be used in other recipes.

Anyway, take ½ cup of Soap Soup and your two juices, and combine for Phase B. Separately, measure out and combine the ingredients in Phase A. Then, in two small pots over hot water, bring both phases to a slow simmer.

Now add Phase B to A gently, *stirring by hand.* As the two phases are mixed together, you'll get a thick and creamy (almost curdly) product at first, then suddenly it will thin out and become very white. Don't be alarmed; what's happened is that the emulsion "switched" in midcareer, from a water-in-oil to an oil-in-water product, really fascinating to watch!

When this second stage is reached and the emulsion is white and lotiony, take your cream off the heat, switch to your electric beater and begin beating at medium speed for about a minute. Then pour your cream (about a cup and a half) into jars.

As soon as you can handle the jars (but while they are still quite hot) give each about thirty shakes, and *then set them aside. Don't pick them up or fiddle with them now for twenty-four hours.* They need this much time to set up into a firm "vanishing" cream with a crystalline structure (thanks to the stearic acid) that will "break" smoothly on your hand when you apply it.

49

If, like Pandora, you just couldn't keep your hands off the jars and your cream doesn't set up properly, don't give up. Simply reheat, rebeat, repour—and use more self-control!

If finding both pineapple and papaya juice stretches your resources too far, you can make a very fine cream with either one or the other. Just make sure you have half a cup of juice in all. And if you just want a down-to-earth "everyday hand cream" without all the drama of natural fruit juices, use natural *water* instead (½ cup) and your cream will still be a thing of beauty and a joy forever. In this last case, though, you may want to perfume it a bit, since you won't have the luscious fragrances of the fruits to perk it up.

Teas and Herbs

PROBABLY the single most trusted ingredient in old cosmetic—and medical—formularies was the dried leaf or flower or root of an herb, or "simple," which when steeped or boiled, became a tea. Teas for drinking, teas for poultices, teas for steaming, teas for scenting, teas for dabbing or washing, teas for rinsing, teas for tanning or bleaching, soothing or stimulating—the list is endless. Modern science respects teas, too: comfrey tea, with its allantoin, is a proved healer and skin-cell proliferant; leaf tea (our regular drinking tea) contains tannic acid, a prime burn remedy.

Here are some cosmetic recipes based on teas and herbs. Some may surprise you!

Double-Zing Herbal Astringent

> 4 tablespoons tincture of chamomile (see "Tinctures as Perfumes" section, page 120)
> 1 teaspoon tincture of benzoin (available in drugstores)
> 3 tablespoons witch hazel
> ¼ teaspoon powdered alum (also at your drugstore)
> 1 pinch dried sage

Dissolve the alum in the witch hazel, then add all the other ingredients and set aside for a few days. Then strain through the foot of an old clean nylon stocking. Makes about ½ cup.

If you really want sparkling clarity, give Double-Zing a "polish filter": Cut a circle out of "wet-strength"-type paper toweling and fold it across, then across again into the shape of an ice-cream cone. Now open the cone, holding two of the folds together so that you end up with a funnel shape, *but without a hole at the bottom*. Then carefully pour your tea *through* it. A paper coffee filter will work, too, if you have one on hand.

Double-Zing feels wonderful, smells wonderful, and really wakes up your skin, toning and tightening. It's a mild antiperspirant too (thanks to the alum), so you may like it especially in the summertime, as an afterbath splash, or as a really tingly refresher for tired, hot feet. *And* it will keep almost indefinitely without refrigeration.

LABEL: *Keep away from eye area.*

"Mother" Herbal Face Gel

> 1 cup boiling water
> Herbs of your choice—enough to make a quadruple-
>   strength (4x) tea
> 1 teaspoon granulated tapioca

Simmer ingredients together until the tapioca swells and begins to dissolve. Then strain through an old clean nylon stocking foot, and allow to cool and to set up to a gel.

You can make as many different herbal gels as there are herbs or combinations of herbs. And they are fascinating! Like masks, they can be applied and left on for treatments, then rinsed off with clear water. If you have trouble spots or teen-age miseries, dab them where the trouble is; they're clear and won't look awful. The tapioca that does the gelling is itself a demulcent, soothing to inflamed skin. I like using licorice for the tea—*very* soothing. As a matter of fact, I like licorice! But try peppermint too, for zing. Or chamomile. Or comfrey. Or golden seal. Or all of them mixed together!

Another licorice recipe that you—or your teen-agers—may enjoy is

Licorice Face Pack (Teen-Age Delight)

> 1 cup boiling water
> Licorice root—enough to make a 4x tea
> 1 tablespoon rice vinegar
> About ⅓ cup fuller's earth (get it from your druggist)

Boil the licorice root in water (or, if it is in tea bags, steep it) until a strong tea (with a heavenly aroma) develops. Add vinegar. Then cool to lukewarm and *slowly* add fuller's earth until you have a smooth paste. Use as a treatment mask. It's especially good to teen-age skin, soothing and drawing and drying for blackheads, oily pores, and pimplets.

Unisex Aftershave

PHASE A (THE "MOTHER"):
  2 tablespoons 4x tea
  1 tablespoon chamomile extract (see below)
  ¼ cup 70 percent ethanol alcohol
  1 tablespoon glycerine

PHASE B (THE FRAGRANCE):
  Pinch of dried tarragon
  3 cardamom seeds, crushed
  1 bay leaf
  ¼ teaspoon Grenadine syrup
  ¼ teaspoon peppermint extract

PHASE C:
  Enough 70 percent ethanol alcohol to make 1 cup total
  1 drop green food coloring
  1 drop blue food coloring

Make 4x tea by steeping 4 teabags in one cup boiling water and squeezing them hard before discarding them; this makes a fine strong astringent tea that will give a good feel to the aftershave and help soothe "razor burns" and nicks.

Next, add your chamomile extract. If you couldn't buy any at your drugstore, soak 1 teaspoon dried powdered chamomile flowers (chamomile tea) in ⅓ cup of 70 percent ethanol alcohol overnight (in a closed jar, or there'll be none in the morning), then strain and "polish-filter" as described in Double-Zing Herbal Astringent. You've thus extracted some of the azulene, the oil that gives chamomile its soothing qualities.

Now add alcohol and glycerine to this, and mix thoroughly. This is another "mother" of aftershaves—a base to which you can add any number of scents. But the one given here (Phase B) is so marvelous that I call it Unisex, because I make it for my husband and steal it for myself! Try it—you'll find that it smells delicious. The procedure is this: Add the Phase B ingredients to "mother" and let the whole mixture stand overnight. The next day sniff it (heavenly!), then strain and "polish-filter" it as already described.

The result should be sparkling clear and scrumptious-smelling. Now all that's left is to add enough 70 percent ethanol alcohol to your mixture to equal one cup in all, and try to make away with it before your husband does! Or maybe, if you're *really* mated, double all quantities and make 2 cups.

Super "Father" Aftershave

¼ teaspoon Dispersible Lecithin (see recipe, page 113)
¼ cup 70 percent ethanol alcohol
2 tablespoons 2x chamomile or comfrey tea (see below)
½ teaspoon glycerine
¼ teaspoon peppermint extract
1 drop blue food coloring
Few drops perfume (see below)

This is another "in original container" recipe, providing you've got a clear glass bottle (3- or 4-ounce). Measure the Dispersible Lecithin and the ethanol alcohol into the bottle and shake together until clear. If necessary, you can shake the bottle under warm running water to help the Lecithin blend in. Brew your chamomile or comfrey tea double strength, to get more of those active ingredients—the soothing azulene of chamomile, the healing allantoin of comfrey. Then add 2 tablespoons of this tea to your mixture, along with the glycerine, the peppermint extract and the food coloring.

You now have a super "mother" (or "father") aftershave *base*. And it's your turn to be creative!

Aftershave is a two-purpose product. It should soothe and tingle after the wear and tear of shaving, and it should *smell good*. In your bottle you have about a third of a cup of superb smoothing and tingling liquid. Now try perfuming it with a recipe from the "Natural Perfumes" chapter, or with ingredients from the candle supply store, where dozens of different perfume oils are for sale at reasonable prices. You can use them pure or mix them to your own taste. Another source of interesting sniffing is the world of food extracts (orange, anise, tangerine, lemon, peppermint, rum) or even liqueurs. Go wild—the wilder the better, if you've got the man for it. Or simply put in a bit of your own—or his—favorite store-bought fragrance.

Conditioning Aftershave

PHASE A:

    2 tablespoons 4x tea

    1 tablespoon 2x tea

    ¼ cup 70 percent ethanol alcohol

    1 tablespoon glycerine

    ¼ of a ½-oz. cake of USP camphor (not mothballs!)

PHASE B:

    2 tablespoons witch hazel

    ¼ teaspoon tincture of benzoin

    1 tablespoon fresh *Aloe vera* gel (see below)

    ¼ cup 70 percent ethanol alcohol

    2 drops blue food coloring

Make a quadruple-strength solution of your own tea-bags-for-drinking tea (which contains tannic acid, the active element in many burn remedies). Add a tablespoon of the double-strength chamomile (or comfrey) tea you brewed for Super "Father." Dissolve the camphor in the alcohol, then add that and the other ingredients of Phase A to the teas. (The USP camphor *must be* the kind bought at the drugstore in ½-ounce cakes—not the kind that discourages moths; it has healing, soothing powers and an intriguing fragrance.)

At this stage, you may like to add your own personal touch—brandy or rum extract, tobacco tincture, a drop of vanilla extract or other spices—to develop a distinctive aftershave flavor.

Let Phase A stand a day or two, then strain and "polish-filter" as described in the recipe for Double-Zing Herbal Astringent.

After filtering, add the ingredients in Phase B. If you don't have an *Aloe vera* plant on your windowsill or don't live in Florida (where it grows everywhere) or can't buy an *Aloe vera* leaf in your health food store, try substituting one tablespoon Slippery-Elm Gelée (page 106) or sprinkle in a pinch (about ¼ teaspoon—

no more or your aftershave may jell!) of the pectin you can buy at the supermarket for making jellies.

Shake together, and *voilà!*—you've made about a cup of a beautiful, smooth, clear face-saver, both soothing and tingly, and as personal as *you* for the man in your life who deserves it.

LABEL: *Keep away from eyes.*

Mink-Sesame Suntan Lotion

PHASE A:

¼ cup mink oil
¼ cup sesame oil
1 tablespoon liquid lecithin
2 tablespoons lanolin

PHASE B:

¼ teaspoon borax
⅓ cup 4x tea

Warm Phase A together and mix until clear. This mixture is the same as Mink-Sesame Suntan Oil (page 63).

If you've been letting your tea bags steep in boiling water while you took care of Phase A, you've now got a nice, strong tea. Add the borax, making sure the tea is still hot. If it isn't, warm it up again so that both phases are the same temperature. Then *slowly,* little bit by little bit, beat B into A. Use your electric beater on high speed (one blade) and really do it right, adding a tablespoon or so at a time and "smoothing out" the emulsion before you add the next one. Your reward will be a smooth, rich emulsion, tan in color, elegant in feel, and *high in sunscreening properties.*

Of all the natural oils, mink has the highest sunscreening ability, sesame is next, and tea, with its tannin, is not only a sunscreen but a burn soother too. So combining them is blockbusting—as good as you can get with natural ingredients. A caution, though: this is *not* a "total sunblock." So if you've got the kind of skin that burns if you just look at it, don't count on Mink-Sesame to do the whole job for you. *Normal* skins, though, on normal days with normal care will find it just wonderful! Needs no refrigeration.

The Richness of Oils

O I L S probably take honors as the oldest cosmetic in the world. Some scholars believe that makeup first functioned as a way of camouflaging the primitive hunter, or in religious ceremonies—to delight or fool the gods. Whatever the reasons, we do know that earth or vegetable colors were mixed with oils and applied to the skin many thousands of years ago.

Some sensuous primitive must eventually have noticed how good he felt afterward; oil on the skin soothed it, protected it from the drying effects of cold and sun, made it feel and look better. By the time of the first Egyptian civilization, five thousand years ago, oils and unguents were favorite cosmetics—and how the Egyptians loved their cosmetics! Archeologists have found them in the Pyramids, still in their elegant jars and bottles, still brightly colored, even still fragrant! Cleopatra, by all accounts, was no beauty, but she knew how to wear a wig, apply kohl to her eyes, and scent herself regally like the empress she was.

The Bible tells us about oils, too—for cleansing, anointing, and perfuming. Alcohol-based perfumes and soap for washing are johnny-come-lately inventions.

Within the last few years there's been an exciting renascence of interest in oils. Body oils, perfume oils, cleansing oils, and various sensuous rubbing oils are suddenly appearing everywhere. On food shelves too, where "oil" used to mean either olive oil, corn oil or "salad oil" (usually a conglomerate), new oils are blooming all the time. Walnut, apricot-kernel (persic), safflower, sunflower, avocado, peanut, mink, wheat-germ, what have you—the list keeps growing, and the cosmetic possibilities keep burgeoning.

Each oil has its own personality, its own special qualities. Animal oils (or fats), such as mink oil or lard or lanolin, penetrate best and hold moisture to the skin. Since they are most like our own skin fat (sebum), they manage to slip down around the hair follicles and do some deep work where it does the most good. Mink oil especially is light and odorless, beautifully emollient, and—surprise! —the best sun block among the natural oils, so it's especially useful in sunburn products. Fish oils, such as cod liver oil, are rich in vitamins and minerals, though they have a strong odor. Vegetable, fruit, and nut oils, and their name is legion, include safflower (polyunsaturated, medium heavy), sunflower (lightest of all, also unsaturated), apricot-kernel or Persic (rich yet light, emollient), wheat-germ (rich in vitamins, also a sunscreen), avocado (buttery rich), peanut (a good, dependable "workhorse" for all formulas), cottonseed (useful, light, penetrating), boiled linseed and castor oil (dry to glossy "film" on the hair). Finally, mineral oil, which is a byproduct of petroleum, doesn't penetrate at all and therefore is perfect for products you want to *slide off* your skin, like cleansing creams, baby oil or mascara remover.

Fats and oils keep fairly well, but they can go rancid eventually, if left open to the air, so I generally like to keep the products made from them in the refrigerator, where they stay fresh and sweet for a long time.

Here are some lovely oil recipes, starting with a historic one—the classic variation on the very first cosmetic cream.

Basic Cold Cream

PHASE A:
¼ cup beeswax (not any other kind of wax, but beeswax, found in Catholic church candles or candle supply houses)
¼ cup olive oil
¼ cup *heavy* mineral oil

PHASE B:
¼ cup plus 2 tablespoons water
½ teaspoon borax

PERFUME:
4 drops citronellol (get it at your drugstore) or your choice

Melt the beeswax and the olive oil together in a double boiler or over water until they are blended (see Beeswax Base, page 92). Then add the mineral oil.

In a second small pan bring the water and the borax to the same temperature as the oils and wax (barely a simmer). Now add

Phase B to Phase A, beating at medium speed with electric beater (one blade). Keep stirring until the mixture is barely warm to the hand. Then add the citronellol, or any other perfume oil of your choice. Pour your cream—which is still thickly liquid—into a jar. Don't worry about it from this point on; it will set up overnight and will start thickening as soon as you give up and leave it alone.

This recipe has really stood the test of time! It was—*sans* borax and mineral oil—the recipe the Roman physician Galen first used around 130 A.D. to make a cleansing cream that felt cooler and more elegant on the skin than plain oil or the greasy unguents used until then (hence the name "cold cream"). With the addition of borax and the substitution of mineral oil for some of the more expensive olive oil, his recipe was used unchanged for 1,800 years, right down to the 1930s, when more "modern" light creams began to take over. It's *still* fine for removing makeup and dirt, will last forever without refrigeration, can be perfumed or colored to suit your fancy, and will really be appreciated backstage at any school theatrical your kids happen to take part in.

This cream is an emulsion—a mixture, like mayonnaise, in which water droplets are permanently dispersed in oil, so that both liquids combine to do their work better. In this emulsion two clear liquids marry and form a white, soft, elegant cream—really an exciting bit of magic every time you do it!

Mink-Sesame Suntan Oil

¼ cup mink oil
¼ cup sesame oil
1 tablespoon liquid lecithin
2 tablespoons lanolin

Warm all ingredients together to melt the lanolin and help thin out the liquid lecithin. The result is a homogenous golden-tan liquid oil that's perfect for keeping you smooth and uncrispy when you sunbathe.

Mink and sesame are the two strongest absorbers of the ultra-

63

violet (burning) rays of the sun among the "naturals." Both of them are highly unsaturated, which means they don't leave an oily feel on the skin, but seem to soak in when you apply them. And both mink and sesame are marvelous emollients. The lanolin and the lecithin are both beautiful moisturizers—that is, they help oils to take in and hold water to the skin. And the lecithin, besides its other goodies, gives Sesame-Mink beautiful spreadability—important because if your suntan oil doesn't spread evenly you'll end up with a blotchy tan at day's end.

A word about sun, which is one of man's—and woman's—best friends, but can also do you in where beauty is concerned. Dermatologists tell us that most skin "aging" is due to the sun's rays. They point (figuratively) to the skin on your buttocks or belly, where the sun never shines: much younger, much less dried and wrinkled than the skin on your forehead—true or false? So our grandmas were right when they ventured out with summertime parasols and gloves—and their skin showed it. We've made a fetish of tans and by so doing may have doomed ourselves to older, uglier skins.

That's why it's important not to burn yourself to a crisp when you sunbathe, and *always* to wear some protective cream or lotion. Mink-Sesame is very good, as is its "baby," Mink-Sesame Suntan Lotion (see recipe, page 58), but neither of these is a *sunblock* (total screen). To get total blocking you'd have to go to ingredients which are not available to home cosmetic chemists (and which are not naturals).

Incidentally, if you do burn, in spite of all precautions, the best remedy I know *is* a natural: fresh *Aloe vera* gel scraped from the inside of an *Aloe vera* leaf and applied as needed. It's worth growing this sturdy plant on your kitchen windowsill just to have it available for all sorts of burn emergencies. And it makes a lovely addition to after-sun cosmetics!

Liquid Brilliantine

"MOTHER":

  3 teaspoons sesame oil
  2 teaspoons castor oil
  4 teaspoons mink oil
  3 teaspoons liquid lecithin

PLUS:

  ¾ cup *light* mineral oil
  A few drops rose perfume oil or your choice

Simply mix these oils together. You now have one cup of sparkling-clear, golden Liquid Brilliantine more luxurious than anything of its kind on the market. It gives ultimate sheen, is a marvelous grooming agent, and contains polyunsaturated oils for conditioning those frazzled ends. The castor oil, a "drying" oil, gives "set"—that is, a "crust" which holds the hair in place after combing. If your hair's a casualty of too much bleaching or permanent-waving, try Liquid Brilliantine under a hot cap, and expect miracles; you won't be disappointed. And, wonder of wonders, that little bit of lecithin makes it easy to wash out! When you shampoo, *this* mixture just floats away with the suds. Leave out the lecithin, and you'll need twice as many latherings to get your hair ungreased again.

Notice that part of Liquid Brilliantine is a "mother." If you're interested in hair products, make doubles or triples of this "mother" and then use it in the two following recipes, Two-Layer Hair Groom and He-She Hair Groom Lotion.

Two-Layer Hair Groom

  ¼ cup Liquid Brilliantine "mother" (see above)
  ¾ cup 70 percent isopropyl alcohol
  3 drops chlorophyll solution (available at health food stores)
      or 1 drop green food coloring

Combine all ingredients in a tightly closed bottle a bit larger than one cup (8 ounces), so that you have room to shake. Now *shake hard*, as you would salad dressing, until the oil and the alcohol seem to combine.

After a few minutes at rest, however, you'll see that two layers form—one bright green, the other clear sparkling yellow. The top layer contains *most* of the alcohol, all the chlorophyll and *some* of the oil. The bottom layer contains *most* of the oils, the lecithin, and a *little* of the alcohol. That is, a little of the oil and a little of the alcohol *transfer*; the rest separate out again.

You've seen these two-layer products on the market before, and now you've made one! There's no cosmetic premium to the "layered" look, but it *is* pretty. And when you shake it up, it will delight you as an alcoholic hair dressing which gives sheen and set without greasiness, nourishes the hair, and even has a bit of hidden interest—the chlorophyll, which combats any tendency to hair odor that you may have. It can be perfumed too, at the rate of a few drops of perfume oil or ¼ to 1 teaspoon of your favorite cologne or perfumed bath oil per cup.

LABEL: *Shake before using.*

He-She Hair Groom Lotion

PHASE A:

½ cup Liquid Brilliantine (see recipe, page 65)

PHASE B:

¾ cup water
¼ teaspoon borax

Heat the water in a double boiler (or over hot water in your electric fry pan) until it reaches a simmer. Then stir in the borax until it is dissolved.

Now add Phase A in a slow steady stream, beating constantly with your electric beater until all the oil has been accepted into the water phase and a smooth emulsion forms. *Don't stop beating.* Take the mixture off the heat and allow it to cool, beating all the way down to body temperature.

You now have a cup and a quarter of smooth, golden hair groom, light and nongreasy. A little bit of this goes a long way, but you'll use a lot, as it really is good for men and women—even for nongreasy kids!

Why does a little bit of water and borax make such a difference between rich, oily Liquid Brilliantine and this elegant light lotion? It's old Dr. Galen's cold-cream magic transferred to another product—the difference between an oil and a cream, or why mayonnaise is different from salad oil and eggs: the emulsion. In this product the oil droplets are enrobed in water, to form a cooler, milky product. (Milk itself is an oil-in-water emulsion.) In mayonnaise the opposite kind of emulsion is formed: the *water* is enrobed in oil, with egg yolk as an emulsifier to help it stay together.

In this recipe the borax and the lecithin are emulsifiers. And lecithin comes from egg yolk. So don't look blank the next time somebody asks you why He-She Hair Groom is like homemade mayonnaise.

Potpourri Bath Oil

- 6 tablespoons apricot-kernel (persic) oil
- 2 teaspoons liquid lecithin
- 1 teaspoon orange extract
- 1 teaspoon brandy extract
- 4 teaspoons rose extract

Shake all ingredients together in a closed bottle (the 10-ounce size is about right).

This is a *floating* bath oil, which means it clings to your skin as you get out of the bath water. But while you're soaking it also cheers your nose with one of the most heavenly scents you're ever likely to soak by. Potpourri is especially nice in winter, when body skin tends to be dry and itchy. But it can do its magic any time. Enjoy!

LABEL: *Shake before using.*

Lemon Throat Stick

PHASE A:

   ¼ cup lanolin
   2 teaspoons solid vegetable shortening
   2 tablespoons peanut oil
   1 tablespoon household paraffin

PHASE B:

   2 tablespoons glycerine
   2 tablespoons fresh strained (or reconstituted) lemon juice
   3 tablespoons water
   ½ teaspoon lemon extract

Combine all the ingredients in Phase A and, separately, all the ingredients in Phase B, using two small enamel pots. Then warm both pots over hot water (an electric frying pan is just right for this). They should be just warm enough so that the paraffin wax stays melted. If you see wax beginning to coat the sides of the A pot, turn up the heat of the frying pan a little.

Now slowly add B to A, beating as you go. When you have a smooth mixture, pour it into a closed jar. Then *shake* and *keep shaking*. At some point, as it cools, it will suddenly and dramatically "set up" to a solid.

If you're interrupted for any reason during this shake/cool procedure, and you find that your mixture has cooled and separated while you were gone, don't panic! Simply rewarm and start patiently reshaking and recooling until you get it right.

You should now have enough solid cream to load into two or three empty stick-deodorant or stick-perfume cases that you've carefully cleaned and hoarded. First make sure the bottom of the case is as low as it can go, then load away, pouring Throat Stick in warm, or scraping in cold with a spatula. When you turn the case up, out will come Throat Stick.

If you have no empty stick cases, you can use Lemon Throat Stick straight from the jar, but it's not as dramatic. The massage action of the stick against your throat stimulates, too. Massage *up*, not down—or follow the lines on your throat firmly, as though you were ironing them.

The lanolin and the glycerine are marvelous moisturizers, the peanut oil and the shortening are emollients. The lemon adds astringency and gives Throat Stick an acid pH. Besides, it smells delicious!

Golden Eye Cream

PHASE A: LECITHIN BASE (see recipe, page 114)
> 5 teaspoons liquid lecithin
> 5 teaspoons apricot-kernel oil
> 2 teaspoons lanolin
> 2 teaspoons paraffin wax

PHASE B:
> ½ cup Soap Soup (see below)

Make Soap Soup as described on page 112 or, if you're using just a little bit for this recipe, as described in Pineapple-Papaya Paw Cream (page 48).

Measure out the paraffin wax by melting the wax first, then heating your measuring spoon in boiling water before dipping out each teaspoon of wax (or just hold the measuring spoon in molten wax). That way, the wax won't congeal on the spoon and you won't lose any.

Now melt Phase A ingredients together over simmering hot water. In a second pot let your Soap Soup heat to the same temperature. Then slowly add the Soap Soup to Phase A, stirring constantly with your portable electric beater at medium speed. When they are thoroughly mixed, take the pot off the heat and keep stirring, allowing the mixture to cool. When it starts to thicken, you can stop stirring and just give it a hand stir once in a while (to keep the emulsion together). When it has cooled to room temperature, pour into jars.

This smooth, lovely golden cream is rich in humectants and emollients. Pat it around the eye area before bedtime, or use it wherever fine lines threaten to get not so fine.

Rich Moisture Cream

PHASE A:
> 2 tablespoons Beeswax Base (equal parts of beeswax and
>   olive oil; see recipe, page 92)
> 1 tablespoon lanolin
> 1 tablespoon liquid lecithin
> 3 tablespoons sunflower oil
> 2 tablespoons unsalted butter

PHASE B:
> 2 teaspoons glycerine
> ¼ teaspoon borax
> ⅓ cup water

Combine all the ingredients in Phase A in one small enamel pot, and all the ingredients in Phase B in a second pot. Now heat both pots over water (a large electric skillet is great for this) until both are at a simmer.

Very carefully add Phase B to Phase A in a slow steady stream, beating all the time with one blade of your electric beater. Keep beating until a smooth thin emulsion forms.

Take your mixture off the heat, and keep stirring, slowing down a bit as the mixture cools, to avoid whipping air into the mixture, but stirring all the way. When the cream has cooled to body temperature, it will be rich, golden, thick and exquisite—a night or throat or eye or elbow cream *extraordinaire*.

While you're doing all that stirring, you might marvel briefly on how cosmetic companies manage to get *their* creams (made in huge vats of anywhere from 5 to 1,200 gallons at a clip) to behave well every time. To make such batches successfully (and identically) day after day, with the same thickness, color, pH, everything, giant machines must record and control the process at every moment. Each of their jars will turn out identical, predictable. Each of yours will not.

So love your failures (when you have them) as well as your successes; you're human, after all. And those enriching ingredients are still in there—maybe seeping out occasionally, but ready to do you good. Use them up and try again. Practice makes perfect (creams).

Rich Moisture Cream has wonderful creative possibilities. Substitute safflower oil or apricot-kernel oil and get a slightly heavier cream that's also slightly cheaper to make. Or try sesame, wheat-germ or mink oils for their sunscreening properties. Mink, especially, gives a silky, special feel. Unsalted margarine could be used in place of butter, again for economy. And for the ⅓ cup water, try substituting an aqueous fruit or vegetable juice (not too acid), like cucumber, peach, apple, or papaya (for its papain—the digesting enzyme which is used in meat tenderizers and will also help tenderize *you*).

Nuts and Seeds
and Grains

W H Y are nuts, seeds, and grains important as beauty ingredients? For one thing, because almost every natural oil of importance comes from this group. Safflower, sunflower, sesame, wheat-germ, avocado, apricot-kernel, walnut, corn, peanut, even coconut oil— almost all the oils we call "vegetable" are in fact expressed from a nut, a seed or a grain.

And since these are the germinating parts of the plant, they are full of vitamins. A chief source of vitamin E, in fact, is wheat-germ oil. Many contain high-quality proteins as well. And some grains, like barley and oats, contain demulcent materials—soothing and healing to your outsides and to your insides as well.

So here are some recipes utilizing the many goodies that seeds, nuts, and grains offer. Use them well! In addition, have fun with all the "vegetable" oils from this group and others that pop up in the chapter called "The Richness of Oils."

Easy Beer Shampoo

    ¾ cup beer (any brand)
    1 cup inexpensive shampoo (supermarket house brand is fine)

Boil the beer over a direct flame until it reduces to ¼ cup. Cool this brew and add it to 1 cup of any inexpensive shampoo. You now have a "treatment" shampoo with some very real old-time virtues: the proteins from the malt and hops in the beer are "substantive" to the hair—that is, they coat it and build it up and help repair damage. Curiously, the beer leaves no odor on the hair, but does do quite a job of beautifying and bodying.

Mmmrrr Perfumed Body Oil

"MOTHER"

- ½ teaspoon lanolin
- ½ teaspoon liquid lecithin
- 1 tablespoon coconut oil
- 2 tablespoons sunflower oil
- 1 tablespoon sesame oil

FRAGRANCE (VARIABLE):

- 1½ teaspoon rose extract
- ½ teaspoon anise extract
- ½ teaspoon rum extract
- ¼ teaspoon peppermint extract
- ½ teaspoon apricot extract

Warm the "mother" oils together gently, stir until sparkling clear, then remove from the heat and allow to cool. If you're too eager to get the fragrance in, it may waft away in steam, so make sure the oil base is at body temperature before you add the rest of the ingredients. Then pour into an elegant bottle—this product really deserves it!—and shake energetically, and an opaque emulsion will form. It will be fairly stable, but if you keep Mmmrrr for a long time, you may need to shake it once or twice to get it together again before you use it.

But you *won't* keep it for a long time. You'll rub it on yourself, your friends, your dogs, your cat—anybody and anything you want to smell and feel scrumptious. And then you'll close your eyes and smile and whisper, "Mmmrrr."

LABEL: *Mmmrrr.*

Colloidal Bath Soak

- 1 tablespoon quick oats (1–5-minute kind)
- 2 tablespoons quick barley (10–12-minute kind)
- 1 cup water

1 tablespoon Dispersible Lecithin (see recipe, page 113)
2 more cups (hot) water

Simmer the oats and the barley together in the first cup of water for fifteen minutes. Then remove what is now a porridge from the heat, and add the tablespoon of Dispensible Lecithin.

Now quickly add 2 cups more of very hot water, stir briskly, then strain through an old clean nylon stocking. Squeeze all this mixture through the foot of the stocking, to get out as much of the goodness of the grains as you can. Then cool and bottle. Makes 2½ cups.

This is a beautiful bath soak for dry, itchy skin. The barley and the oatmeal soothe and soften, the lecithin is emollient and enriching. Try giving it as a gift to geriatric friends or relatives who suffer from "old-age skin" and watch them come back for more. And when they do, surprise them! Using Colloidal Bath Soak as a "mother," brew up a batch of even richer and creamier Colloidal Bath Oil.

LABEL: *One cupful per tubful.*

Colloidal Bath Oil

2½ cups Colloidal Bath Soak (one whole batch, see recipe above)
1 tablespoon liquid lecithin
2 tablespoons Soap Soup (see recipe, page 112)
2 tablespoons sunflower oil

Warm together over low heat the Soap Soup, the liquid lecithin, and the sunflower oil. As they come to a simmer, beat at medium speed, and a smooth creamy lotion will form.

In a second pot, heat the Colloidal Bath Soak to about the same temperature. Now add ½ cup of the Soak to the lotion you just formed, pouring in a slow stream and beating as you go. When the mixture is smooth and thin, reverse the process and slowly pour the *lotion* into what's left of the *Bath Soak*, again beating as you go until the final mixture is beautifully smooth.

Colloidal Bath Oil is gloriously rich, smooth, and luxurious, a treat for the skin. It disperses when you first put it into your bath water; then a few minutes later the oil portion surfaces to coat *your* surface, while the oatmeal and the barley do their work under the waves. If you like Colloidal Bath Soak, you'll love Colloidal Bath Oil. It's worth the extra effort to get all that luxury—and it's better than anything I know on the market.

You might like to perfume this and make it even more wildly sybaritic. If you do, add the perfume after the final step, when the Colloidal Bath Oil has cooled down to warm.

LABEL: *½ cupful per tubful.*

Milk, Cream, Butter,
and Yogurt

F R E S H dairy products—milk, cream, butter, yogurt—are treasured additions to any cosmetic for the same reason they're welcome in your diet: they're rich in protein, vitamins, and fat, all of which add to skin health and beauty. No doubt you've seen the shelves full of commercial cosmetic products proudly announcing they're made with milk. They generally contain low-fat dried milk for the most part—and though they do benefit from some of the goodies milk has to offer, think how much more you could get when you make the same kinds of products with fresh whole milk, or even cream!

Emperor Nero's beautiful second wife, Poppaea Sabina, used a mask made of ass's milk, flour, and honey to keep wrinkles away. In fact, the lady was so fond of bathing in pure ass's milk that when she traveled, three hundred she-asses went along with her just so that she could "draw her bath"!

Gossip was that Cleopatra too bathed in milk to beautify her skin. And a famous old Indian love manual (the *Ananga Ranga* from about 450 A.D.) advised brides "suffering from spots" to rub their faces with sesame, white mustard, ground caraway, and milk for one week, and "on the wedding night the skin will be as pure and flawless as white snow on the mountains."

Anna Held, the famous Ziegfeld beauty, took milk baths, too, to turn her skin to silk and her public to jelly. So you, dear reader, would do well to treat this chapter with respect!

Remember, though, that milk recipes are highly perishable, so make up small amounts fresh every week or two and *keep them refrigerated*.

You may also like to try substituting milk for water in some of the other recipes in the book, to give richer products. Be careful, though—don't make this switch in recipes with acid ingredients, or you may end up with a cosmetic cottage cheese!

Peaches-and-Cream Facial Cooler

> 2 tablespoons light cream (or half and half)
> 2 tablespoons fresh strained peach juice (no sugar added!)
> ¼ cup plus 2 tablespoons 4x tea
> 3 tablespoons witch hazel

The best way to get your peach juice is to put a whole ripe sweet pitted peach through your electric juicer—if you have a juicer. Failing that, you can rice a soft peach or chop it in the blender and strain the resulting mush carefully through an old nylon stocking, discarding (or eating) the pulp. The messiest way, but one that will also give you peach juice, is to grind it in a meat grinder (set in a roasting pan so that the lovely juice that drips down doesn't get away).

However you obtain it, *mix* the light cream and peach juice at room temperature. Then, stirring steadily, *slowly* add the tea. When the tea is all in, add the witch hazel *slowly*, still hand-stirring constantly until the batch is uniform and smooth.

You now have a lovely, fragrant cooling lotion, beautiful for the skin. Use it in hot weather by patting it into the skin like a facial. It will stimulate and refresh you and, as a bonus, provide emolliency, vitamin-A and -D content, and protein richness.

You have many interesting choices for the tea portion of this recipe: peppermint for added zing, chamomile for soothing and healing, regular tea for its astringency, or you choose it. In any case, Peaches-and-Cream is exotic enough, delightful enough, and easy enough to warrant many repeat batches.

Cucumber After-Sun Cooler

> 2 tablespoons whole milk
> 2 tablespoons strained ground cucumber juice (peel and all)
> 2 tablespoons 4x tea
> 2 tablespoons witch hazel

With all ingredients at room temperature, mix the milk and the cucumber first by hand, then add the tea slowly, and finally the witch hazel, stirring all the way.

This process must be *slow*, and the stirring must be constant, so that the milk doesn't curdle, but accepts both the tea and the witch hazel without putting up a fight. Your patience will be rewarded by a soothing, cooling after-sun lotion, smelling deliciously of cuke, and carrying the benefits of milk, the mildness and skin-softening of cuke, and the burn-soothing tannin of tea.

As with Peaches-and-Cream Facial Cooler, you have all the world to choose from in the use of various teas. I like regular tea because of the burn-soothing tannin content, but it does rather spoil the beautiful green color that develops otherwise from including the cuke peel in your juice. Grind the cuke in an electric vegetable juicer (if you own one), or in a blender (cut into cubes), then squeeze through a nylon stocking. If you really want to develop that green, cool color, use peppermint tea, and then, on really hot days, smooth Cuke Cooler all over your body—and *glow*.

Eggnog Body Lotion

¼ cup peanut oil (or any other light oil)
2 tablespoons whipped margarine
2 whole eggs
½ cup plain yogurt
¾ cup fresh whole milk
¼ cup witch hazel
1 cup fresh-strained, canned, or frozen apple juice
1 teaspoon rice vinegar (or any mild vinegar)

Warm the margarine gently and mix with the oil. Cool that mixture back to room temperature before adding the eggs. Just stir them in by hand until smooth. Now, stirring constantly with your *electric beater*, add the other ingredients *one at a time*, making sure each is thoroughly accepted by the liquid before going on to the next. When you are finished, you'll have about 3 cups of smooth, elegant Eggnog Body Lotion that is so good you'll never want to be without it again! It boasts the skin-loving proteins of egg, milk, and yogurt, the soothing pectin from apple juice, the acid pH contributed by the apple juice and the vinegar, the refreshing astringency of the witch hazel, and vitamins galore.

I sometimes add a bit of cinnamon to this lotion; it gives a most provocative fragrance! Or if you really want to stay in the eggnog tradition, try a bit of grated nutmeg and rum flavoring. Get creative with the oils, substituting luxurious oils such as mink or apricot-kernel, or sunflower, safflower, corn, or whatever others your health food store has to offer. You can also try some juice substitutions, and see how you like the results. This recipe as it stands, though, is my absolute favorite. And this, together with the variation below (which creates an absolutely marvelous bath oil) can't be bettered, in my view, for using, giving, and sharing. They're better than anything I've ever bought, and I can't praise them highly enough. The only warning I must give is: they're practically edible, and therefore *refrigerate!*

LABEL: *Shake before using.*

Eggnog Bath Soak

    1 cup Eggnog Body Lotion (recipe above)
    1 cup fresh whole milk

Simply shake these together, pour about a half cup into your bath, and prepare to feel like Cleopatra. It's a rich dispersing bath oil that first mixes with the water in your tub and then sends part of its emollient goodness back up to the surface, to coat you as you exit. Glorioski! *Refrigerate.*

LABEL: *Shake before using.*

Strawberry-Yogurt Facial Mask

    2 tablespoons All-Purpose Clay Mask (see recipe, page 100)
    1 tablespoon plain yogurt
    1 tablespoon fresh strained strawberry juice (may be made
        from frozen strawberries)

Stir ingredients together by hand and apply to your face when you have fifteen or twenty minutes to lie down quietly, feet up, and think beautiful thoughts. Then rinse off with cool water, in a circular motion. A washcloth is good for this, or just your hands, or try it before your shower so that you can just rinse it off under the running water. The mask is nondrying, so it won't flake off all over as you rest and cogitate. What it *will* do is cleanse and stimulate, give a pH treatment, cool and astringe. And that's not bad for "strawberries and yogurt"!

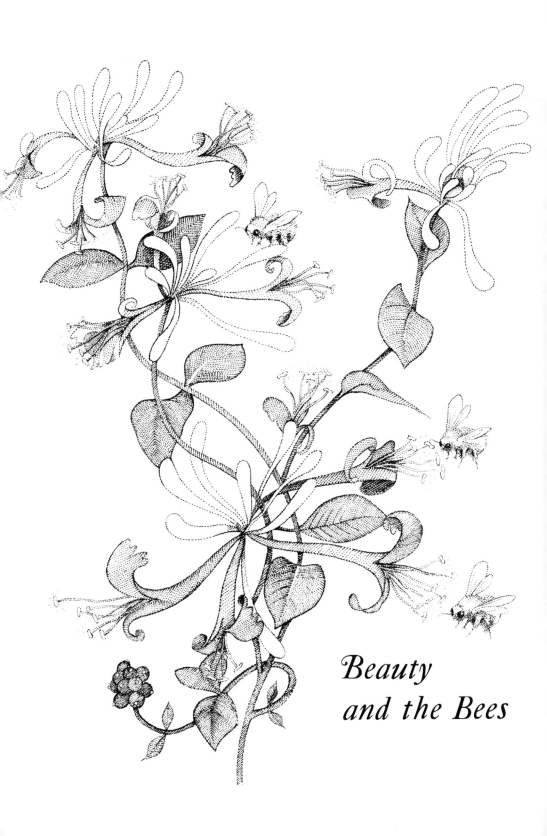

*Beauty
and the Bees*

Y O U have, of course, noticed honey and beeswax cropping up in these pages with fair regularity. Both, supplied by hard-working bees, are magnificent cosmetic ingredients, and have, in fact, been used in cosmetics since cosmetics were born.

Honey is the earliest known humectant, and still one of the best. It holds moisture to the skin, never spoils or sours, and has a thick, syrupy consistency that can make cosmetics feel rich and heavy. (It can also make them feel sticky and gooey—but the recipes in these pages prevent that.)

Why is moisture-holding so important, anyway? Dr. Irvin H. Blank of the Harvard Medical School hung pieces of callus (hardened skin) in various oils and in water and discovered that oil-soaking of skin doesn't actually soften, while water-soaking does. Dr. Blank reasoned that it is loss of water that toughens skin; therefore, holding water *to* the skin (moisturizing) will keep it softer and more pliable. And that, of course, is what we all want!

Honey can also clarify soap, making it transparent. Honey is high in vitamin content, and is mentioned in the old cosmetic formularies as a skin purifier and nourisher. So, for any or all of these reasons, it certainly belongs on the shelf of any natural cosmeticook.

Bees make the honey from the nectar of flowers, and while they are at it they also make the package for honey—the beehive. The building material for the hive is a waxy substance, yellowish or brownish in its natural state, melting only at high temperatures. This last means that it's valuable for candles. (Imagine making a candle with something with a *low* melting point, like tallow; you'd have a pool of oil—which is exactly what a tallow lamp is like.)

In cosmetics, beeswax imparts a stiffness and drag to lipsticks, gives elegant "break" and stiffness to creams (when you rub them on, there's a definite moment when the cream suddenly "melts" and goes gliding onto your skin), acts to stiffen or "body" throat sticks, creams, hair straighteners—any product where this special texture is essential.

The beeswax you'll buy will probably be bleached white and made into religious candles; Catholic churches insist on beeswax (from virgin bees) for their altars. But you can also come by it in sewing stores (as a thread stiffener), in candle supply stores, or, of course, from your local beekeeper.

When I was a little girl we used to chew beeswax-and-honey —pieces of actual honeycomb as the bees made it. Maybe kids still do. We thus got the beauty benefits of the honey inside and the stimulation of the beeswax on jaws, gums, and teeth. Now I confine my beeswax to the outside of me, though I confess I still manage to eat up an awful lot of my "cosmetic" honey!

Milk-and-Honey Mask

> ¼ cup *strong* fennel tea
> ¼ cup milk
> ¼ cup honey
> Half of a 1-ounce package of pectin (supermarket)

Mix the tea, the milk, and the honey together to form a homogenous mixture. Then sprinkle in the pectin as you slowly beat with your electric beater. Make sure the pectin is accepted completely, and the mixture smooth, before you stop beating. Put the gel that results into a jar and let it stand overnight to "swell."

You now have a mild, elastic milk-and-honey mask that will spread lusciously on your face, treat you to the proteins of milk, the "smoothening" of pectin, the humectants in honey—and maybe even the first aid for wrinkles attributed to fennel by the old, optimistic herbalists.

Hot Honey Facial

> 1 tablespoon Lecithin Base (see recipe, page 114)
> 1 tablespoon honey

Melt the ingredients over hot water, stirring, until you have a clear gelatinous solution. Remove from the heat, pour into a wide-mouthed jar, and allow to cool.

When you have at least fifteen minutes alone, get out your Hot Honey Facial, heat the jar over hot water, and slather on as hot as you can take it. Let all that goodness work into your skin while the warmth lasts. When it has thoroughly cooled, wipe it off with clean tissues, then cleanse off the last bit with cold Apple Cheeks Toning Lotion (page 42) or any other good astringent.

The combination of oil, lanolin and lecithin in the Lecithin Base, and the smooth humectant honey is marvelous for you. And, finally, patting with cold, astringent Apple Cheeks leaves you glowing and rosy. An unexcelled beauty treatment for tired skin. Try it!

Avocado Honey Mask

    1 tablespoon mashed avocado
    2 tablespoons raw honey
    2 egg whites, or 1 whole egg

Blend together in electric blender, or whip until smooth.

This is the mask to blend up and pop on when you're baking a soufflé and making an avocado salad (not a bad supper!) and happen to have a bit of avocado and two egg whites left over, plus ten minutes to think beautiful thoughts while the soufflé rises and the avocado marinates in dressing. Avocado Honey Mask is creamy, luxurious on the face, tightening (thanks to the egg whites) enriching (honey) and hard to wash off, so better use it before you dress up in all your finery. But it's fun—and refreshing—and you can eat what's left of the mask, and plant the avocado pit! Waste not, want not.

Golden Scarecrow Beauty Drops

    1 egg
    2 tablespoons sesame oil
    2 tablespoons honey

Separate the egg, drop the yolk into a small jar, then add the sesame oil and the honey. Hand-stir until thick, rich, and smooth. Now add the egg white, close the jar, and *shake hard*. The mixture will thin out somewhat and become even smoother. And so will you, when you dab it on in dry-skin or wrinkle areas—throat, elbows, upper lip, and especially those nasty crow's-feet around the eyes. You wondered why I called this "Scarecrow," didn't you? Try it, and you'll find out!

Beeswax Base

> ¼ cup beeswax
> ¼ cup olive oil

Measure the olive oil into a Pyrex measuring cup, then add enough chipped beeswax (beeswax is *hard*) to bring the level up to ½ cup. You've now added ¼ cup beeswax. Set the measuring cup in very hot water in your electric fry pan and carefully stir until the wax and the oil are thoroughly melted together and all the wax has dissolved. Pour into a wide-mounted jar and allow to cool.

You now have a soft "mother" base that is much easier to measure than beeswax itself, will keep indefinitely, and can be used wherever equal parts of beeswax and oil are called for. Naturally the base can be made with other oils too, by the same method, and the results will be the same.

Easy Lip Gloss

> 2 teaspoons Beeswax Base (see recipe above)
> 6 tablespoons mink oil

Melt the ingredients together over boiling water until they're thoroughly "married." Then pour into your prettiest small jar and let cool.

This is a lip pomade of truly awesome glossiness and emolliency. It can make you look more kissable, or it can do harder work and soothe and smooth chapped or dry or sunburned lips.

If you have an old worn-down lipstick, try digging a small

chunk of it out of the case to add to the Lip Gloss while the latter is still hot. Mix this color in well, and you'll instantly have tinted lip pomade, shiny and pretty. You can use it as a cheek-glosser too! And if those are not enough uses for one recipe, try using Easy Lip Gloss (untinted!) as a superconditioning hair pomade. Just take a wee bit on your fingertips, spread it thoroughly on your palms, and apply palms to hair. You'll need only the littlest bit to go a long, long way.

Solid Brilliantine

PHASE A:
    1 teaspoon beeswax
    2 tablespoons mink oil
    1 tablespoon lanolin

PHASE B:
    2 teaspoons water

PERFUME:
    5 drops orange extract
  10 drops rum extract
  10 drops anise extract

Measure the ingredients of Phase A into a wide-mouthed glass jar. Then melt them together over hot water until they are thoroughly dissolved and the mixture is homogenous and clear.

Now remove the jar from the heat, add the water, close the jar tightly, and *shake hard*. Keep shaking as the mixture cools and the water is absorbed (emulsified) into Phase A.

Just before the mixture goes solid, add the perfume ingredients, shake or stir again, and that's it; your Brilliantine is done.

This is a rich hair dressing with sheen and elegance to make your frazzled hair look beautiful. It can also be used as a "pressing oil" for hair straightening if that's your thing. And it smells delicious!

No reason why you couldn't load it into an empty stick-deodorant case just before it cools to solid form. Turn the case all the way down, push the Brilliantine in, trying not to leave air pockets, and let it cool thoroughly until solid. When you turn the case up, a "stick" glides out.

Beeswax Wrinkle Thing

> 2 tablespoons beeswax
> ¼ cup plus 1 tablespoon mink oil
> ¼ cup plus 1 tablespoon liquid lecithin
> 2 tablespoons lanolin

Combine all the ingredients in a wide-mouthed glass jar. Then warm them over hot water until they melt together thoroughly and form a homogenous clear liquid. When this cools it will turn into a rather stiff cream, similar to petrolatum, but with a warm, lovely amber color and remarkable richness and emolliency.

I call it Wrinkle Thing because there are a million uses for it; whatever part of you needs "oiling" will soak it up. Dry or damaged hair will accept it gratefully, and you can add it to your hot cap treatments for extra penetration. I even use it to enrich old, dry leather (the comparisons are obvious!) and have saved some treasured old handbags and waterlogged shoes that way. You'll find uses, too, by the bushel, once you realize how good and nourishing this is. Try it, under gloves, as a night hand treatment. Or use it as an eye cream, elbow cream, heel cream, knee cream . . . Need I say more? It's fabulous!

RICE STARCH

Good-Earth
Products

S o m e of us find it surprising that beauty products can come from what we were brought up to call, inelegantly, "dirt." "Dirt" was to be avoided at all costs, "dirt" meant bad, "dirt" was a dirty word! It was an age when washing was hard and "dirt" was responsible for mysterious diseases that crippled children overnight. (Infantile paralysis came from "dirt," I was taught.)

And yet radium came from "dirt," minerals were mined from "dirt," salt, clay (for masks, which even *my* mother used), talcum powder, alum (for pickling), even diamonds (which nobody scorned) came from "dirt." In fact, all the minerals and nutrients that encouraged plants to grow, all the strength that eventually finds its way into our bodies, originates, if you think about it, in the "dirt."

Primitive civilizations seem to know this in their bones, and intimately connect themselves and their lives not with a sentimentalized symbol of Mother Earth so much as *dirt itself.* They use it to draw the soreness out of insect and snake bites, to cool inflammation, to paint themselves and their possessions, and as building blocks for their homes.

We too have something to learn from "dirt," and if you don't believe it, here are some marvelous Earth Products to cool you, smooth you, soothe you, beautify you, and make you feel and look—clean!

Instant Perfumed Bath Powder

> 2 cups plain talc (drugstore)
> 10 to 20 drops of your favorite perfume or scented bath oil

Simply put the talc into your blender, turn the blender on first at low speed, then gradually increase to highest speed. When it is whirling smoothly at highest speed, you'll find that you can take off the blender cover without making clouds of dust. Have the courage to do this and drop in, slowly, a bit of your favorite perfume. Replace the cover and let the talc whirl for a bit more. Then turn the blender off, and *presto!*—elegant perfumed talcum

powder. If you'd really like to feel good about this recipe, check
the cost of the body powder sold under your perfume's brand
name. Quite a saving, isn't it? And every bit as good for after-bath
smoothing.

B.A. Baby Powder

- 1 teaspoon cod liver oil
- 1 tablespoon zinc oxide powder (drugstore)
- ½ teaspoon liquid chlorophyll (health food store)
- 2 cups talc

Put the talc and the zinc oxide powder into your blender,
and blend first at slow, then gradually faster and faster until you
are at highest speed. Take off the blender cover—you already know
the talc won't fly around—and add the cod liver oil drop by drop,
blending as you go. When the mixture is absolutely blended and
smooth, you have a fine "treatment" baby powder, wonderfully
soothing to sore little bottoms, helpful when diapers are smelly,
and vitaminized with vitamins A and D (cod liver oil) to help
healing. It even smells like a very famous, and very good, baby
product, which is no accident at all.

"Smooth All Over" After-Bath Powder

- 1 tablespoon *isopropyl* alcohol
- ½ teaspoon lanolin
- ½ teaspoon mink oil (or wheat-germ oil)
- 2 cups talc (drugstore)
- ½ teaspoon of your favorite perfume

Put the alcohol, the lanolin, and the mink oil into a baby-food
jar, close the jar, and heat the mix over hot water (or *under* hot
water) until the lanolin melts. Then shake the jar to mix well, and
let cool. You'll have, at this point, a milky-looking dispersion.
When the dispersion is cool, open the jar, add the perfume, and
shake once more.

Now put the two cups of talc into your kitchen blender. Turn the blender on slow speed first, then gradually increase the speed until it is at the highest setting. When the talc is swirling around this fast (and thus won't fly out all over your kitchen), take off the top of the blender and, while the talc is still swirling, *slowly* pour in the milky dispersion of alcohol, oils, and perfume.

After a few minutes of this blending, the alcohol will evaporate, and the rich oils will be smoothly dispersed in the powder, coating each particle individually.

This is a truly luxurious body smoother and is a special favorite of mine. I especially enjoy buying myself something frivolous with the difference between the cost to me of "Smooth All Over" and what I would have paid for the commercial body powder that smells just like it. *Mmmmm.*

Jogger's Deodorant Powder

> 2 teaspoons alum (drugstore; its official name is ammonium alum NF)
> ½ cup talc
> ½ cup cornstarch (or rice starch, if you can get it)
> 1 teaspoon chlorophyll
> ½ teaspoon peppermint extract
> 1 tablespoon isopropyl alcohol

Dry-blend the talc, the cornstarch, and the alum in your blender, starting at low and gradually increasing to highest speed. (For this product, a blender isn't even necessary; a martini shaker will do, or even an old glass jar that you can shake and roll around enough to blend the powders thoroughly.)

Now dissolve the peppermint extract and the chlorophyll in the alcohol, and slowly, blending all the way, add this to the powders. Then blend a bit more just to make sure everything is thoroughly mixed.

This is a fine deodorant foot powder, underarm powder, afterbath (or on-the-trail-when-there's-*no*-bath) powder that will keep indefinitely, zing a little coolness at you when you put it on, and help to protect you from chafing and rashing when you work up a "perspire." If you can locate some rice starch, use it instead of the cornstarch; it's even smoother, softer, and more absorbent. The alum and the chlorophyll work on body odors, and the talc, as always, is valued for its extraordinary silky feel and "slip."

If you'd like to perfume this one or make it more "female," add a bit of perfume oil at the same time as the chlorophyll-alcohol mixture (use a blender for this if you do it) and the scent will be "accepted" smoothly.

Mother Mask Base

"MOTHER":
  ¾ cup water
  ¾ cup glycerine
   1-ounce package dry pectin (supermarket; for making jellies)

Mix the water and the glycerine together. Then, with your electric mixer at high speed, slowly sift in the powdered pectin, making sure that it's smoothly accepted by the mixture before you stop beating.

You now have a rather stiff gel. Put it aside and let it swell further overnight before using it in any other recipes.

All-Purpose Clay Mask

  2 tablespoons Mother Mask Base (see recipe above)
  2 tablespoons kaolin (or "china clay"; available at your drugstore)
  ¼ teaspoon peppermint extract

Simply mix these ingredients together. You've made a thick, nondrying clay mask, similar to masks you buy for many dollars. Apply it generously to your cleansed skin with a spatula or your fingers, and let it work for about fifteen minutes. Then rinse it off with cool water, working it out and off the skin with your fingers in a circular motion. Your skin feels cool, tight, and bright—thanks to the humectant glycerine, the drawing action of the clay, the smoothening pectin, and the zing of the mint.

LABEL: *Keep away from eye area.*

Very Special Oatmeal-Honey Mask

¼ cup All-Purpose Clay Mask (see recipe above)
  1 tablespoon honey
  2 tablespoons oatmeal "brew" (see below)

Cook a few tablespoons of oatmeal (any kind) in water, following package directions. While it's still warm, strain and squeeze it through an old, clean nylon stocking to get the thick glutinous "brew." Discard the oatmeal husks (and maybe the stocking too!) and combine this warm brew with the honey. (You may want to warm your mix a tiny bit more if the honey doesn't go in smoothly.) Now, with a broad knife or spatula, "cut" and mix the oatmeal-brew/honey combination into the All-Purpose Clay Mask until smooth. If you have trouble working the ingredients together, try adding a bit of witch hazel, which will help.

Use this in the same way as All-Purpose Mask. It has the same delightful effects, plus the added soothers in the oatmeal, the vitamins, and the moisturizing magic of the honey.

LABEL: *Keep away from eye area.*

Oily-Skin Treatment Pack

½ cup fuller's earth (drugstore)
  2 tablespoons witch hazel
  1 tablespoon isopropyl alcohol

Mix the witch hazel and the fuller's earth thoroughly. Then add the isopropyl alcohol, and mix again. If you like, you can adjust the amounts of witch hazel or fuller's earth to get exactly the degree of thick smoothness you like best.

Apply the mask to clean skin, and leave it on until it dries and "cracks." Then remove with cold water, rubbing it lightly with your fingers in a circular motion. Repeat this treatment twice a week for super-oily teen-age skin.

The fuller's earth has a marvelous ability to absorb oil, the witch hazel tightens pores, the alcohol is drying. All in all, it's just what your skin needs if pimplets, blackheads, and yawning pores are the bane of your existence.

LABEL: *Keep away from eye area.*

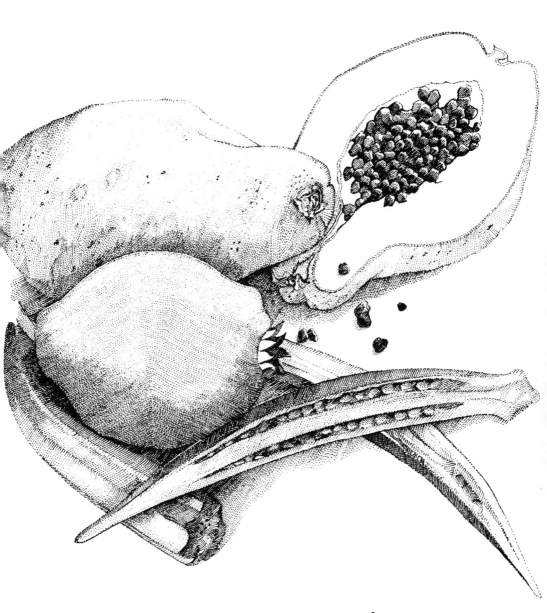

*Gums and Thickeners, or
How to Make Milk into "Cream"*

T H E obvious reason for caring about gums and thickeners in cosmetics is that you want what you *put* on to *stay* on and not trickle down your face and moisturize your chin! This sounds frivolous, but think about it. One of the most important qualities of a cosmetic is that it stay in place where it will do you the most good. Whether it be a lipstick, an eye cream, or a suntan, a "penetrating" oil or a hair groom, *you* put it there, but it's got to stay there on its own. And so, unless its function is washing, quick-splashing, or instant toning (like skin toners, astringents, aftershaves), it should *not* have the consistency of water.

And that's where gums come in.

Part of the art of cosmetic formulating is to get just the right thickener for each job—tacky if you need that, smooth and unctuous if you need that, gelatinous, stiff, with or without "break." The more interested you get in making your cosmetics aesthetically satisfying as well as effective, the more important the thickeners become. In a way, they are what makes a cosmetic a cosmetic; anybody can slap cucumber juice on her face, but when one learns to modify it, mix it, combine it with other goodies, and then thicken it so that it stays where it belongs, lo and behold!—Cucumber Cooler.

Commercial cosmetic formulators care a great deal about the *appearance* of their product, so they make sure that qualities like texture, feel, viscosity, color, and clarity are as "on target" as they can make them. Natural thickeners are rarely used. Instead, cosmestic chemists employ synthetics (mostly cellulose derivatives) to do the job, because these are more or less inert and won't react with the other ingredients in the formula. The only naturals you'd be likely to find in a commercial product are quince-seed mucilage, gum karaya (in wave sets), carrageenan, or perhaps gum tragacanth.

But you, with infinitely more time and money to spend (per jar, of course!), have the whole range of natural thickeners to choose from: tapioca, okra (yes!), slippery elm, gelatin, pectin, natural waxes, starches (corn, rice, potato), as well as quince seed, and the other gums such as karaya, tragacanth, and arabic. And you'll think of more as you try them!

These natural gums sometimes react with, or cause reactions in, other ingredients in your formula, so you do have to keep an eye on how you use them. Protein gums tend to curdle in the presence of alcohol, for instance. But if you use the recipes here as a first try, and *then* go off on your own when you need to, you shouldn't have much trouble. And you should come out with real natural *cosmetics*—not just a slice of raw potato or a dab of lemon juice, but the genuine article. So thicken away!

Slippery-Elm Gelée

This is strictly a "mother" base for use in other recipes, and yet—feel it, smell it! It's lovely. No reason not to use it on your face as a mild, mild mask or pat it on to "set" your makeup. Another useful trick: it tends to stabilize lotions. So if you've got one that's separating mysteriously, try working in a bit of this Gelée.

> 1 tablespoon slippery elm (health food stores; the very fine shredded kind is best, without large pieces)
> 3 tablespoons water (or, for much more elegance and "softening" action, papaya juice if you can get it)

Cook the ingredients together over boiling water for thirty minutes. Then filter through an old nylon stocking, squeezing out every bit of the precious juice. It will thicken and gel on cooling.

Newfangled Glycerine-and-Rosewater Gel

PHASE A:
> 2 tablespoons 70 percent *ethanol* alcohol
> 1 teaspoon powdered pectin (supermarket)
> ½ teaspoon rosewater perfume (drugstore)

PHASE B:
> 2 tablespoons witch hazel
> 2 tablespoons glycerine
> 2 tablespoons water

COLOR:

    2 drops food coloring

Separately, mix the ingredients in Phase A and Phase B. You'll notice that the pectin powder will not dissolve in the alcohol of A, but don't worry. That's exactly what you want. Later, when you add B, the pectin particles will swell smoothly, forming your gel.

Add A to B, stirring continuously with your electric beater until the mixture thickens a bit. Drop your coloring in at this time, too, if you want some (blue is "cool," red is more traditional). Now pour the product into a jar to cool.

Come back and admire it in about an hour. It will have formed a beautiful, sparkling-clear hand and body gel that is good for chapped lips or hands, dry skin, or scaly skin, and is windburn- or sunburn-soothing. The pectin (from the rinds of fruits like apples or citrus fruits) is soothing (demulcent) inside or out; the glycerine moisturizes, the rosewater smells lovely. And gelling puts it and keeps it where you want it.

Protein Wave and Nail Set

    ¼-ounce packet unflavored gelatin (supermarket)
    ½ cup water
    ½ teaspoon cider vinegar

Mix the gelatin and the water and make sure that all the granules disappear. It will begin to form a clear gel, but before it actually sets up (and when it has reached the thickness you like) add the vinegar and stir in well. This will retard final gelling. Store it overnight and it's ready to use the next day. Smear it thickly on hair strands before you roll them in curlers.

Unflavored gelatin is an excellent (and economical!) source of protein for the hair or nails. Protein Wave and Nail Set is a versatile product, basically a fine hair-setting lotion, but great for "nourishing" brittle nails, too. While you're waiting for your hair to dry, dab some on your nails; it will set to a glossy film and help both nails and hair to look and feel better.

LABEL: *Keep refrigerated.*

All-Purpose Body Lotion

- 1 egg yolk
- 2 tablespoons sesame oil
- 2 tablespoons honey
- ¼ cup plus 1 tablespoon fresh whole milk
- 2 tablespoons Slippery-Elm Gelée (see recipe, page 106)

Combine the egg yolk (save the white and use it as a mask) and the sesame oil, then add the milk and the honey. If necessary, warm the milk and honey slightly first to make sure all the honey is thoroughly dissolved in. Finally, stir in the Slippery-Elm Gelée, and bottle the mixture.

This body lotion is both emollient and moisturizing; why be content with one *or* the other? It soothes too, and offers the protein and lecithin of the milk-and-egg combination. It's great for all-over smoothing after your shower, or for keeping winter-dried skin moist and supple. If you have a friend in the hospital, try this as a gift for gentle body massage.

If you want to perfume, simply stir the fragrance in last. But the color is great just as is—soft, creamy gold. You can't beat nature!

Other "Mothers"

Newfangled Soap

>   Lots of fat—enough to render down to 6 pounds
>   1 pound lye (flakes)
> 2 ½ pints cold water
>
> PLUS:
>
>   Oatmeal, almond meal, milk powder, cornmeal, honey,
>   whole ground cucumber, etc.

If you're really serious about natural cosmetics and have some time—and fat—to spare, you might like to try making Newfangled Soap. The basis is an old recipe your grandma's grandma used—roughly as follows. Collect fats and oils from any and every source: lard, meat fat left over from frying hamburgers or cut from chops or steaks. If you really want to get fancy, add a dash of olive oil or peanut oil to your fat mixture—but don't be too generous with these liquid fats (oils), or your soap will be soft.

When you've collected all the fat you can stand, slowly render it—that is, simmer it with an equal amount of water until it is clear and all the pieces have boiled to crisps.

Then cool to room temperature (chill or add ice water), until the goopy, chunky fat floats to the top.

Skim off this "purified fat" with a slotted spoon, and throw away all the charred mess at the bottom of the pot.

Then to every 6 pounds of pure fat add one pound of pure lye—*not drain-cleaning solution or powder*, but lye bought at your grocery store or supermarket under that name, for making soap. Dissolve each pound of lye in 2 ½ pints (5 cups) of cold water. Use an enamel pot.

Be careful when you dissolve lye! Lye can heat the water to boiling, and it is really nasty to handle. *Wear rubber gloves!* If you should get any lye on your skin, rinse first with water, then with dilute vinegar until all the "slippery" feeling of the lye is gone.

To make soap, warm your lye solution to about 90° F. and heat melted fats to between 110° F. and 130° F. (not hotter). You can use a candy thermometer for the purpose, to get this temperature just right.

Then slowly, using your best "mayonnaise" technique, pour the lye solution in a thin even stream into the fats, *stirring all the while with a wooden spoon*. If you stir too vigorously at this point, your soap will separate. Remove from the fire and keep stirring slowly until the soap is about as thick as honey. This will take ten or twenty minutes, and at this point it has cooled enough for you to get creative.

Add a bit of any of the ingredients listed above, or any that your heart desires. Add powders, fats, grains, perfume, or food color. Do your thing! The abrasiveness of almond meal, oatmeal, and cornmeal are especially good for scrubbing oily teen-age skin. And you already know the benefits of some of the other suggested goodies.

Finally, pour your soap into molds—into cardboard boxes lined with damp cloths, or into any flexible molds such as candle molds, small jelly molds, etc. (You might try greasing a mold that isn't very flexible, to help remove the soap later.) In twenty-four hours you can unmold your soap, cut it into cakes if it was in a box, and then hang it in a string bag or nylon-net shopping bag for two weeks to "cure."

Homemade soap makes a unique gift, can save you quite a bit of money (and can save your sink from clogging up with thrown-away fat). But it won't be as white and refined as the kind you buy in the store. Never mind—it's "natural"!

Soap Soup

If you're going to make a number of recipes using Soap Soup, it's worthwhile to make a large quantity and tuck it away (it keeps forever) to have on hand when needed, instead of having to whip it up each time. You'll need:

An 8-ounce-avoirdupois box of *pure* soap flakes (the kind
    that are white and 99 and 44/100ths percent pure)
8 cups water

Bring the water to a simmer (not a boil!) in a big pot, dump in the soap flakes, and stir till clear. Then cool and bottle. Don't worry if Soap Soup clouds or curdles or even gels on standing. Just rewarm and restir until it is clear before using recipes.

If this seems like just too much Soap Soup, make it the very same way using one ounce (avoirdupois) of soap flakes (you'll need a kitchen scale for this) to every cup of water. Or take a small cake of soap of the same brand, read the label to find out how many ounces it weighs, then use the same number of cups of water as there are ounces in the cake. Don't put the soap in all-in-a-lump, though; *shave* it in. Results will be the same as for the larger quantity.

Dispersible Lecithin

This is a "mother" recipe that is useful in any number of other formulas in this book. It's worth making a little hoard, rather than mixing it each time, because liquid lecithin as you buy it in the store (probably a health food store) is soluble only in oil. Dispersible Lecithin is much easier to handle for cosmetics, will dissolve in either alcohol or water-based liquids, and is even useful as a "conditioner" that you can add to commercial cosmetics if you want to. It contributes a rich skin feel and a bit of "slip," besides the protein goodies inherent in egg yolk.

½ cup Soap Soup (see recipe above)
¼ cup liquid lecithin

Measure the lecithin into a wide-mouthed jar, squeegeeing the measuring spoons to get every drop of this honeylike liquid out. Then add the Soap Soup, close the jar tightly, and *shake hard*. Keep shaking until the mixture is smooth and uniform and no dark droplets of lecithin are visible. Warm gently if necessary, to get a smooth mixture.

Dispersible Lecithin will keep indefinitely without refrigeration.

Lecithin Base

This "mother" is a recipe in itself. You can use it as is for a superconcentrated eye cream or dry-skin treatment. It also forms an important part of many recipes in this book. So make up a batch and put it aside. It will keep forever.

¼ cup plus 1 tablespoon liquid lecithin
¼ cup plus 1 tablespoon apricot-kernel oil
2 tablespoons lanolin
2 tablespoons paraffin wax

Warm all ingredients together over hot water until you have a homogenous clear liquid. Make sure that all the paraffin is dissolved and mixed in. Then pour into a jar and allow to cool. It turns into a rather stiff cream (about the consistency of petroleum jelly) with a lovely amber color.

A hint for measuring paraffin wax, which has to be chipped and is a bit hard to handle: Either melt it first and dip it up with a warm spoon (so that the wax won't coat the cold spoon and be lost) or chip it into the already measured liquid—i.e., measure your apricot-kernel oil and liquid lecithin into a measuring cup (5 ounces in all), then add enough chipped paraffin to bring the level of the liquid to 6 ounces, or ¾ cup.

Natural Perfumes

W RITING about natural perfumes pales when you sniff a flower. What perfume anywhere has the immediacy, the distinctness, the distin*ction* of the fragrance that greets your nose when you bend down to a rose or a lily of the valley, or crush a leaf of peppermint between your fingers?

That's not to say, of course, that natural perfumes—or *un*natural ones, for that matter—can't give delight; they do. But it's really not their perfection in terms of the original that you should measure them by. The *blends* of perfumes and other substances that you—or commercial perfumers—make can have a glorious olfactory personality of their own. And you can create, with very little trouble, 100 percent natural perfumes (using natural ingredients only) which do not resemble in any way anything you could bend down and sniff in nature. This doesn't diminish them; in fact, looked at in the light of creative pleasure, it enhances them. You can make smells never smelled on land or sea until you invented them! And they can be absolutely scrumptious. Now, doesn't that make you want to get out your jars and measuring spoons?

Not to be contradictory, there are *some* flower scents which you can approximate pretty well. And these too give enormous pleasure. Rose is one, and it's one of my favorites. Gather ye rose petals while ye may, and in a few paragraphs I'll tell you how to make the best rose perfume you ever met. But lily of the valley— which is also a special favorite of mine—has defied me, and I think has defied commercial perfumers far more expert than I am. You just can't make a lily-of-the-valley perfume from the actual flowers. But there *are* marvelous-smelling lily-of-the-valley–*type* perfumes made from mixtures. Get my point?

Without pushing it too far, I'd like to offer another example, because it's so "in" today, when natural products are getting so much attention and respect. That is the "herbal-blend" fragrance. You can, with dried or fresh herbs, plus anything else you fancy, make marvelous and original herbal fragrances, world without end! And you can *buy* herbal fragrances (some of which are not made from anything that ever grew) which are marvelous. But none of them will smell like what *you* smell when you put your face into a handful of sprigs of fresh-picked herbs. (They may smell, for the most part, *better*. But not the same.)

So don't let slavish copying of natural fragrances be your aim. Don't "photograph"; "paint"! Your pallette is infinite, limited only by your own energy and imagination. Be as free to experiment as nature is. Here's the method. (And if you ever manage to create a "true" lily-of-the-valley fragrance, send me some!)

MAKING PERFUME OILS

This process, known as *enfleurage*, is centuries old and has been practiced by primitive folk cultures, and by the most respected modern perfume houses using tons of elaborate equipment to do essentially the same thing:

Gather petals or flowers without stalks or leaves while they are blooming and before they've begun to wilt at all. (Some old herbals suggest that sunrise is the best time for this; others insist on evening. I suspect that what's important is that the flowers be moist and dewy, not dried out, when they are picked and used.) Put the petals or flowers into a jar filled with bland unscented oil (like peanut, safflower, sunflower, sweet almond) or solid vegetable shortening or lard (melted but *not hot*).

Let the flowers stand in the oil or fat for twenty-four hours. This will transfer the fragrance into the oil. Then strain the oil carefully (warming *slightly* to remelt if it's a solid fat), throw the old flowers away, and replace them with fresh ones. Repeat this process for three or four days, until the oil has the fragrance you desire. You now have perfumed oil.

This oil can be used on your body, and will mix beautifully with your cosmetics if *they* contain oil. Simply include a small amount, perhaps ¼ teaspoon, of this perfumed oil with the oils in the recipe, making sure not to subject the perfume to heat. In fact, a good rule of thumb is to put the perfume in as late in the recipe as possible, but before the product has hardened if it's going to.

There are many "body oils" on the market; with this method you can experiment and create your own. You can't get "natural civet" (which comes from the sex glands of the civet cat), but you *can* extend your range from flowers to herbs, vanilla beans, tobaccos, peels (like lemon, tangerine, grapefruit, lime), barks (cinnamon, sassafras)—anywhere your imagination will carry you.

If you use a solid fat for your *enfleurage*, you can make "solid perfume sachets." Rewarm the fat, put a drop of food color in if you like, pour it into beautiful little boxes, and simply let it cool. This can take care of a whole slew of Christmas presents or party favors, elegantly, originally, and personally. Do make sure that you use a fat that doesn't go rancid; solid vegetable shortening is better for this than any fat you might render yourself, because it's clean, white, and absolutely odorless. (In the perfume trade these solid fats with fragrance are called "concretes" and sometimes sell for hundreds of dollars per pound.)

ALCOHOL-BASED PERFUMES

Make an *enfleurage* as described above, using an oil rather than a solid fat. When your fragrance is at the strength you like it, take an equal amount of 70 percent *ethanol* alcohol (*not* isopropyl, which has a strong odor of its own) and shake them together vigorously in a tightly closed bottle.

Let the mixture stand for a day, then shake again. Do this every day for a week. Then let the fat and the alcohol separate, carefully pour off the alcohol, and behold!—it has "lifted" the perfume from the oil and is itself now an alcohol-based perfume.

Not all of the fragrance has been lifted, however, and so the oil too is still fragrant and can be used with pleasure.

Your new perfume certainly deserves a beautiful (tightly closing) bottle and a special name. It can be dabbed hither and thither on your person as it stands, or it can be used in cosmetics when there's alcohol in the recipe. Make sure that when you use it as an ingredient you don't subject it to heat (which would drive the alcohol off and change your fragrance) and that you put it into the mix as late as possible.

Your natural alcohol-based perfumes are not as long-lived as commercial ones, because all commercial perfumes use fixatives to hold the scent, and often these are not available to home perfumers. However, they often *are* natural—ambergris, from the bellies of whales, for example, or civet, from the wild civet cat of Ethiopia, or musk, from musk oxen originally but now almost always synthesized.

You *can* stabilize your perfumes a bit by adding to them a bit of castor oil or glycerine. Either one will help hold your perfume fragrance on your skin when you use it. But experiment with small amounts; too much will feel tacky.

TINCTURES AS PERFUMES

Both the perfume oil and the alcohol-based perfume described above are *extracts*—that is, the fragrance is extracted from something and lodged in something else. Another kind of perfume (and another kind of extract) is the *tincture*.

Start with 70 percent *ethanol* for this one, and add to it your fragrance materials—tobaccos, leaves, flowers, peels, barks, whatever. These materials should be dried, since water in any amount dilutes the tincture. Use as little alcohol as you can get away with, "wetting out" the materials, mashed up or cut with scissors, in the alcohol in a small, tightly closable bottle. Let this stand a few days, strain off the alcohol, throw away the leaves, and repeat the process, gradually getting more and more fragrance (and color) into your alcohol. When you've achieved the strength you like, your tincture is ready to be used.

Again, you can include this as an ingredient in cosmetics or enjoy it on its own. The fragrance can be made longer-lasting with a few drops of glycerine or castor oil. And it should be kept tightly capped, in a handsome bottle, and named something special.

MORE ABOUT PERFUMES

If you're one of the people who are really turned on by the idea of making perfumes—as I am—there are all kinds of avenues down which you can pursue your interest.

First of all, you should think a bit about what makes a perfume great. Go to the nearest perfume counter and sniff until your nose gets tired. (For the untried nose, this generally doesn't take long; more experienced noses build up more endurance.) Ask yourself about the perfumes you like. What is the first smell out of the bottle, the first to hit you (and usually the first to go). Perfumers call this the "high note." What is the middle range of smells composed of? *Many* notes, each one adding to the whole, each one making the scent more complex, less like a single flower, more complete, "rounder."

A great perfume should be provocatively itself, complex and hard to pin down, with many "notes"—a high that's immediate, a low that hangs on and sustains, and many echoes and reverberations in the middle. In fact, the terminology is like music, and deservedly so; a good perfume is a chord.

Even more, a good or great perfume is personal, individual. To sniff it out of the bottle is to do it an injustice. It literally warms to you; as it lives on your skin, the alcohol evaporates, the oils of the fragrances come alive on you, and the scent takes on a more distinctive character. It *marries* you. So when you make your own fragrance, you want to make something that not only smells good in the bottle but suits *you*—or the very special person you honor when you create a perfume for him or her.

Many natural materials which may not come to mind right

away are marvelous for perfumes when you think about them. Grasses and hays lend fabulous "green" overtones. Brandies and rums, wines, liqueurs (which, after all, are blended for their unique flavor—and isn't smell flavor?), nuts, spices, beans, leaves, skins—the list is endless. Vanilla is marvelous for rounding off a fragrance. Peels such as those of cucumbers contain oils which can, with some trouble, be rescued and used in perfumes. They can be simmered gently in water until the oil appears on the surface; then cool the water, refrigerate, and scoop up the oil. Of course it is a tiny amount—but how precious. And how powerful.

Perhaps a better way of recovering oils, if you own a blender, is to blend the fresh peels with as little water as possible, then refrigerate until the oil comes up and you can take it off. I like this a bit better, because cooking to extract tends to change fragrances. But that may be just what you want. Experiment!

A great source of scents is your druggist, who can probably furnish you with rose-geranium oil (a beauty!), spirits of peppermint, bay rum, oil of cloves, rose soluble oil, lavender, or whatever else he happens to have tucked away in his back room. Try candle stores too (although candle perfumes tend to be somewhat more overpowering), liquor stores (start by asking for grenadine and aromatic bitters), health food stores, supermarkets, any place where you can come by extractable (or already extracted) perfume raw materials. I get so intrigued that I shop for new ideas wherever I go, and find them in the most unlikely places. Half the fun is the finding, so I won't tell you all of mine. But keep your eyes—and your nose—open. You'll be surprised at what lies out there waiting to be discovered!

If you're really going to get hooked by perfumes—and if you've read this far you already are!—buy a fat notebook, call it PERFUMES, and do what the formulators do: keep track of everything you make, everything you buy (where you buy it, what strength, the maker, anything else you find out about it, including how long it keeps its fragrance). Be especially painstaking about keeping track of your original formulas, not only end results but how you got to them—false starts and first steps, little serendipitous pieces of information gleaned along the way that may not have worked for that formula but may someday get you out of a problem in another one. This notebook will make it possible for you to repeat your successes, minimize your failures, remember details that otherwise would get lost in the shuffle, and learn, learn, learn. It also is something to share, if you run across another perfume nut (and you will!) sniffing at a counter or in a back room somewhere.

A small trick that professional perfumers use will save you "nose time." Cut a plain blotter into narrow strips and use these to test your fragrances as they're aborning. Just dip the strip, wave it about a little to get rid of some of the alcohol, and sniff. Then label it, stick it upright in a low jar and keep it for comparison as the work goes on. That way you have a whole record of what you do and what the results are. Otherwise it's almost impossible to remember how a mixture smells, and you have to do it again to smell it again.

Remember to store all perfume ingredients—and, of course, the finished products—in tightly capped jars or bottles. Better still, keep them away from light, and fill the containers as full as you can to keep them away from contact with air. Fragrances are fragile. But, oh, how marvelous!

Here are some recipes for perfumes to get you started. But don't let these be the finish. If you've got the nose for it, press on! The rewards are enormous.

Heritage Lavender Perfume

    4 tablespoons dried lavender blossoms (health food store,
           maybe, or herb store, or mail order)
    4 tablespoons 70 percent *ethanol* alcohol

Soak the lavender and the alcohol together for about a week. (Professional perfumers call this "maceration.") On the last day warm the mix *gently* over hot water (double boiler or electric fry pan), then strain out the wet lavender blossoms. You can do this with a tea strainer, or by the old-nylon-stocking method. In any case, *squeeze out* every bit of the juice you can; it is your perfume! Work quickly, too; alcohol evaporates in air. For really professional results, give your perfume a "polish" filter by straining it through a paper-towel filter or a tightly woven coffee filter, as described on page 53. You will lose a little, but you'll gain "polished" clarity.

This perfume and all other perfumes keep better if refrigerated, though they don't have to be. And for long-term storage of this or any perfume, your freezer will keep a fragrance from "aging" at all. This is a particularly useful bit of information if, despite all your home perfuming, you're tempted by a buy in your favorite commercial perfume. Tuck an extra bottle or a large-size "economy" bottle in your freezer, making sure it's not filled to the absolute top (liquids expand when frozen). When you're ready for it, it will be ready for you.

A more complex and much more interesting natural-perfume recipe is

Elusive Exclusive

- 1 tablespoon dried tarragon
- 3 tablespoons dried lavender blossoms
- ¼ cup plus 2 tablespoons 70 percent *ethanol* alcohol
- 1 teaspoon anise seeds
- 1 teaspoon fresh strained or bottled lime juice
- ½ teaspoon rose extract (from the baking or spice department of your supermarket, or ask your druggist for rose soluble oil)

Macerate, strain and filter as with Heritage Lavender. Makes a dark amber-colored perfume with an indescribable and absolutely marvelous fragrance. When you make this one, *please* think up a better and more worthy name for it. This is the best I could do, but it just isn't fabulous enough!

Bay Rum

This is a version of the classic old aftershave that was slapped on gentlemen's faces in barbershops with striped poles. It can still be found on the market, but usually doesn't hold a candle to its complex and fragrant granddaddy. Here's a version that *your* gentleman may like. You can make it as is or use it as a model for a custom variation that he'd like even better.

5 ounces vodka (90 proof or better)
1 ounce Jamaica rum
   A few bay leaves
¼ teaspoon allspice
1 stick cinnamon
¼ teaspoon orange extract

Put all the ingredients into a bottle with a tight cap and let them stand for about a week. Shake them now and then, whenever you think about it. Then open the jar, strain out all the solids, and polish-filter through paper toweling. You'll end up with about 5 ounces of good Bay Rum (which you can also drink, if that suits you better!).

Oldfangled "Glycerine and Rosewater"

2 tablespoons witch hazel
2 tablespoons glycerine
½ teaspoon rose soluble oil (drugstore)
¼ cup water

Simply shake the ingredients together in a bottle, adding the water last.

This is a very old recipe for a very good hand "lotion." Glycerine is "nature's own" humectant; it holds water in a formula so that it never dries out, and it holds water to *you* so that you don't dry out, either. Witch hazel is astringent and fragrant, and it manages to neutralize the slightly "fatty" sensation sometimes left on the skin by the glycerine. Rose oil plus water can also be bought at your drugstore as *rosewater*. And for a pleasant variation, try orange-flower water instead (5 tablespoons). Chapped hands, rough elbows or heels, dry skin all respond to the gentle comforting of this old-time classic.

Glossary

ALBUMIN   A protein which constitutes about one seventh of the substance in egg white (the rest is mostly water); an excellent emulsion stabilizer (helps hold oil and water phases together); a film former (tightens when spread on the skin and allowed to dry), and therefore useful in facial masks.

ALCOHOL   This is not just "drinking stuff." Chemically speaking, there are many alcohols. Two of especial interest for cosmetic use are *ethanol* (more properly, *ethyl alcohol*), which is usually made by fermentation of grapes or grains, and *isopropyl alcohol*, which also can be obtained by fermentation techniques (natural origin), but in fact is usually made by chemical modification of petroleum. Both of these alcohols are available in your local drugstore or supermarket, at 70 percent strength (the rest is water), for use as rubbing alcohol. Check the label carefully, however; rubbing alcohol is usually 70 percent isopropyl alcohol. It is harder to find the 70 percent ethanol, but at least one national drug chain sells this type of rubbing alcohol. But beware: *No rubbing alcohol is drinkable!*

     Ethanol alcohol was first obtained by distillation of wine in A.D. 900 (by the Arabs), and soon thereafter it began to be used in perfumery. In the Middle Ages it was known as "Aqua Mirabilis" and used primarily for medicinal purposes. In the fourteenth century, an alcohol distillate of rosemary flowers was very popular, under the name "Hungarian water"—which was one of the first "commercial" colognes to be sold. You should know that vodka made in the United States contains (by law) nothing but ethyl alcohol and water—no flavor is added. The percentage of ethanol is half of the "proof" listed on the label; "90 proof" means 45 percent ethanol. Unfortunately, for cosmetic purposes that usually isn't strong enough (perfumes and aftershaves usually have more alcohol content than that). Certain states (Connecticut is one) do allow the sale of pure grain alcohol (ethanol), through liquor outlets, but they charge the usual stiff liquor tax.

You may be wondering, by this time, how drug and cosmetic companies that use alcohol in their formulations manage to get around all the alcohol restrictions. Very simple. They register with the Treasury Department and submit to continual inspections of their plants and records, in exchange for which they are allowed to purchase 90 to 100 percent ethanol (that's 190 to 200 proof!), tax-free, for less than one dollar per gallon. They are paying for only the alcohol itself. *You* pay for the privilege of drinking it, when you pay (including tax) twenty times that for the form called vodka. *Sic semper tyrannis!*

ALMOND EXTRACT Extracted from inedible bitter almonds, not the sweet almonds which are household favorites (and which yield sweet almond oil). This familiar food flavoring makes an excellent perfume additive.

ALOE VERA GEL The gummy substance in the fleshy leaves of *Aloe vera*, a cactuslike plant found in many tropical climates, including Hawaii and southern Florida. When you cut the leaves, the clear gel oozes out. It is used "as is" in cosmetics or occasionally dried to a powder so that it will keep longer. Contains a healing agent of considerable value for burns. The U.S. Navy stockpiled *Aloe vera* at one time for use against the terrible radiation-burn danger of atomic attack. Native Floridians often keep an aloe plant in their kitchen or back-yard garden in case of kitchen burns, or for first aid to visiting relatives who get too much sun.

Mixing fresh *Aloe vera* gel with strong Pekoe tea, plus a bit of powdered Irish moss (to thicken to a gel), makes a handy-dandy home burn remedy.

ALUM   A general term referring to several aluminum salts, all astringent when applied to the skin. Some are so strongly astringent that barbershops used them in "styptic pencils" to stop the flow of blood from shaving nicks. Ammonium alum NF is the mild form we advocate for home cosmetics. It is sold only in drugstores under this name ("NF" refers to purity sufficient for drug usage). This sort of alum is also used for purifying drinking water, for gargling, and in baking powders.

ANISE   Anise seeds come from the dried ripe fruit of a plant known as *Pimpinella anisum* (what a name for the lead character of a comic opera!). Anise oil is extracted from these seeds. Anise extract is made from anise seeds, too, but in an alcoholic base.

ANTIPERSPIRANTS   Should not be confused with deodorants; although all antiperspirants also deodorize, the reverse is not true—plain deodorants do not act as antiperspirants.

Antiperspirants are almost always based on aluminum salts, which act as strong astringents and "close up" the sweat ducts temporarily. These aluminum compounds are also sufficiently antiseptic to kill odor-causing bacteria, thereby also acting as deodorants.

APPLE JUICE   If made from whole apples (peel, seeds, core and all), this is a good source of pectin, a gumlike thickening material which is marvelously useful for making jams and jellies and, of course, cosmetics as well. Pectin (and, therefore, apple juice) is soothing to the skin.

APRICOT EXTRACT   Should really be called "apricot flavor." A concentrate of the fruit itself, sometimes "fortified" by use of synthetics. An excellent perfume additive to "round off" fragrances. Found on the flavorings shelf of your supermarket, or maybe in candle stores as a perfume oil.

APRICOT-KERNEL OIL   Known also as "Persic oil." A smooth, light, richly emollient oil obtained from the kernels that are discarded during the process of preparing dried apricots. Available in health food stores.

AROMATIC BITTERS   These herbal extracts really do have a heady aroma, which you will find intriguing and useful in home perfumes. Use only a dash, just as you would in flavoring a cocktail. Available in food and liquor stores.

ASTRINGENTS   A general class of agents, including (in "strong" versions) antiperspirants. Astringents tend to contract skin tissue, decreasing pore size temporarily, and when strong enough to have styptic action they can coagulate blood. A typical astringent is *Alum.*

BARLEY   A grain which can be steeped in hot water to extract a mucilagenous starchy material which is very soothing to itchy skin. This is what makes "barley water" useful in cosmetics, and especially in bath products.

BATH OILS   These come in two basic types. *Floating bath oils* form a continuous film on the water, which is great when you use them primarily for fragrance purposes. *Dispersible bath oils* go milky when poured into the tub, dispersing evenly throughout the whole amount of water; thus you can soak in them, not just get coated stepping out of them.

BAYBERRIES   The fruit of wax-myrtle trees. The ancient Roman physician Galen (inventor of the "cold cream") said that the leaves and bark of these trees have great healing power. Modern usage is pretty much limited to fragrance applications and to using the wax coating of bayberries in making candles.

BEESWAX   What bees' honeycombs are made of. Commonly, it is purified and bleached from its natural dark-yellow color to waxy white. A mainstay of cosmetics for two thousand years, beeswax is easily emulsified by borax, producing stiff, high-sheen, very stable creams. It can be obtained from beekeepers, of course (they get about a pound of the wax for every eight pounds of honey produced), and from candle supply stores. Religious candles intended for use in Catholic churches must be made only of beeswax (which is produced by virgin bees), and therefore these candles are a convenient source for the home cosmetic chemist. Just break off a small chunk of the candle as needed.

BENTONITE A purified white clay used in cosmetics to thicken lotions and as an oil absorbent (to reduce shine) in makeup products. Soothing to the skin. Swells considerably in water.

BENZOIN Tincture of benzoin (your druggist may call it "compound tincture of benzoin") is an alcoholic extract that's made from the resin of trees of the genus *Styrax* that grow in Siam and Sumatra. It is antiseptic and forms hard films. Mixed with lard or lanolin, it's a useful ointment for minor wounds.

BORAX The alkali of choice in making cold cream (with beeswax, any oil, and water—that's all you need). Chemically, it's sodium tetraborate. Why is it used in cold creams? Because it emulsifies fats—the same reason you put it into the daily laundry. Emulsifying fats means mixing them intimately with water. If you have only a little water (cold creams are two-thirds wax and oil, one-third water—or less) you get a thick water-in-oil emulsion. If you have lots of water, plus soap, as in your laundry washing machine, you get a very thin oil-in-water emulsion; in fact, it's so thin that it just rinses right out during the rinse cycle, and *presto!*—clean clothes.

Your druggist calls borax "sodium borate." Use only USP grade.

BROMELAIN The active-ingredient enzyme in pineapple which gives it skin-softening properties.

BUTTER A lovely fat for cosmetic uses, but unfortunately too expensive for commercial cosmetics. We are so used to using butter only as a food that its ancient history will perhaps come as a shock. The ancient Hindus offered it as a sacrifice in their worship. Greeks and Romans had butter, but didn't eat it, either; they used it only as a remedy for skin injuries or as an ointment for skin and hair. And in Spain butter was sold only in "medicine shops" until as late as the seventeenth century. Perhaps it's time to look at its superb emolliency and light skin feel, its vitamin-A content, its *natural* benefits, and elevate butter once again to a cosmetic ingredient.

CAMPHOR, USP   A compound derived originally from the camphor trees of Java, China, and Brazil (where the trees have to be over fifty years old before they produce it). Seventy-five percent of the current world supply of camphor is now made synthetically. A counterirritant and somewhat anesthetic material when applied to the skin, it also contains significant amounts of azulene, an anti-inflammatory healing and soothing agent.

Do not use any camphor in cosmetics except USP grade, which is obtainable only from drugstores. It usually comes in cellophane-wrapped half-ounce cakes. Although real "camphor balls" were once used as moth preventatives, in general mothballs sold today are not camphor. Most mothballs contain "para" (paradichlorobenzene), *a chemical which must not be used on the skin under any circumstances.*

CARDAMOM   The spice sold for cooking purposes is the dried ripe seed of a plant called *Elettaria cardamomum*; the oil from these seeds is used in perfumery.

CASTOR OIL   One of the few natural oils which are alcohol-soluble. Extracted from castor beans (the oil is also known as "oil of *Palma Christi,*" if that makes you feel any better about it), castor oil is used by the ton in resin and fiber manufacture, in detergents, and in cosmetics. The purgative use *you* know about is one of its lesser uses. Most lipsticks contain large percentages of castor oil (it's a good solvent for the dyes).

Emollient castor oil has been used for dry-skin conditions, and also (mixed with cornstarch and zinc oxide) in baby ointments.

It has been used for forty or fifty years in hair grooms, where (because it is a semidrying oil) it forms a tough shiny film—almost a crust—considered very desirable for certain types of men's products.

An herbal hair tonic recipe known to old-time druggists as "bitter oil" called for one ounce of rosemary, a half ounce of nettle, two ounces of sage, one ounce of olive oil, one ounce of castor oil, and one pint of 50 percent (100-proof) ethanol. The dried herbs were ground and soaked in the alcohol for about a week, then strained, and then the oils were added and just enough water to produce a slightly milky look.

CHAMOMILE A thick bushy plant with yellow flowers. A light blue oil known as azulene (see also *Camphor, USP*), which is known for its healing properties, can be extracted from the flowers. Chamomile's medicinal action has been heralded for over 2,500 years. The azulene reduces swelling (antiphlogistic action) and has a reputation as an anti-irritant (in products such as shaving creams, depilatories, etc.) and a bactericidal as well. Tea made from chamomile leaves is used as a blond rinse in northern Europe; that's probably how Debussy's "Girl with the Flaxen Hair" got that way.

CHLOROPHYLL The vital factor of all plant life, with a function similar to that of hemoglobin in our blood. In fact, the chemical structures of chlorophyll and hemoglobin are almost identical, varying only in that the blood factor is built around an iron atom, while chlorophyll is built around a magnesium atom.

The chlorophyll solution sold in your local health food store is extracted from alfalfa. Well known for its deodorant properties, it is also a lovely leaf-green dye and has been incorporated in ointments which are used for reducing swelling and pus formation, and to promote healing of wounds.

COCOA BUTTER A cream-colored fatty wax which melts at body temperature, obtained from roasted seeds of the *Theobroma cacao* plant. Chocolate bars (white or brown) are primarily cocoa butter plus sugar and vanilla flavoring. Cocoa butter is an excellent lubricant for massage purposes, and many soaps contain it as a "super-fatting agent" to make them feel richer and milder on the skin; in creams and lotions it serves both as an emollient and as a soft wax.

COCONUT OIL   A substance expressed from the kernels of the seeds of the *Cocos nucifera* tree (the coconut palm). It is not at all related to cocoa butter. A white, semisolid lardlike fat, it is so stable to air that it will remain bland and edible for several years without refrigeration. An excellent cosmetic emollient for creams and lotions, for body oils, and in soaps and shampoos.

COD LIVER OIL   This has been used in burn remedies and in a soothing ointment applied to many generations of newborn infants. (Melt equal parts cod liver oil, lanolin and petrolatum together, then blend equal parts of that mixture with zinc oxide. If it seems to need stiffening, add a bit of beeswax.) Cod liver oil contains significant amounts of vitamins A and D, both of which are of value in skin treatments.

COMFREY   An unusual plant. Its large hairy leaves are prickly and cause the skin to itch; the young leaves are tender, however, and are occasionally cooked as a vegetable by country people. It is the roots which are most interesting to us—full of a glutinous juice known for centuries to have mysterious healing powers for fresh cuts, wounds and bruises. We now know why: *Symphytum officinale*, as the plant is called officially, contains allantoin, an ingredient much prized in cosmetics for its cell-proliferation ability —it helps wounds to close faster and in general helps skin renew itself.

CORN OIL   Obtained by wet milling of corn grains, this is one of the "heavy"-feeling vegetable oils. It has a fairly high unsaturate content.

CORNSTARCH   This too is obtained from grains of corn as a water extract. Cornstarch contains amylose and amylopectin. The starch powder alone may be dusted on the skin, or it may be first mixed with talc. Cornstarch is sometimes dissolved in lotions or directly into bath water, to reduce dry-skin itchiness.

CORN SYRUP   A syrup containing corn sugar (primarily dextrose), which has some natural humectant properties.

COSMETIC   From the French *cosmétique* ("beautifying") and before that from the Greek *kosmetikos* ("decorating"). The legal definition speaks of preparations for a beautifying purpose (in contrast to drugs, which have a therapeutic purpose).

There is an old French saying which goes: "There are no ugly women. There are only women who do not know the use of cosmetics."

COSMETIC CLAYS   These come in two types: those which swell in water and those which do not. Those which do swell ("hydrate" is the technical term) are used in masks, and also to thicken makeups and to suspend color pigments. By the way, cosmetic clays are white, not like your garden-variety type of dirty old mud.

The swelling varieties include bentonite and kaolin, both of which absorb oil and are used in makeup products to reduce shine; bentonite is used in lotions as a thickener, and kaolin (also known as "china clay") in dusting powders to promote adherence to the skin. The nonswelling clays include fuller's earth, used primarily for its absorbent qualities.

COSMETIC COLORS   These are either *dyes* (soluble in either water or oil) or *pigments* (insoluble). Cosmetic paints of various sorts, such as berry juices and earth colors, have been used since prehistory. Cro-Magnon and Neanderthal graves show evidence that ocher (an iron ore) was apparently used on the face and body even in that early period. Greek women in Xenophon's time used white powder on their faces, but unfortunately they used lead carbonate, which gave rise to occasional unexplained cases of lead poisoning. Today we still use face and body paints, perhaps more subtly, perhaps not. Most of our dyes are now synthetic (including all the so-called "food colors"); but perhaps the main difference is in shade styles. For instance, in their cosmetics the ancient Phoenicians used indigo (which they obtained from a delicate shrub that grew on the shores of the Mediterranean), but we don't like blue lips—*this* week!

CUCUMBER For cosmetic use this should always be juiced peel and all. Using the peels adds beautiful green color and a lovely fragrance (which you would otherwise lose) to the juice. Cucumber juice contains a skin-softening enzyme (erepsin) similar to papain, the enzyme used in meat tenderizers. This is apparently the basis for cucumber's long history of use in cosmetics. Cucumber juice spoils *very* quickly (even in the refrigerator), so make it fresh in small quantities, and expect that cucumber cosmetics won't keep long, either.

Alcoholic cucumber-juice recipes abound in early cosmetic literature, serving as skin fresheners, skin toners, and astringents. The alcohol helps to preserve these products. When mixed with fresh buttermilk, cucumber juice has been used as a skin bleach, and also to prevent nail-splitting.

DEODORANTS Materials which, one way or another, kill odor-causing bacteria. *Fresh* sweat is odorless and inoffensive. The "sour" odor developing under arms is the result of bacterial action, which occurs incredibly quickly. Body odors of this type can be prevented quite simply by putting an antiseptic on the area (the underarms), thereby killing the odor-causing bacteria.

DRY SKIN Has fine pores, is slightly tight, and has a scaly appearance (under a magnifying glass) and a tendency to redden and wrinkle. It suffers from a lack of both fat and moisture.

EMOLLIENTS Generally oily materials, but they need not feel greasy. They may, and often do, feel velvety smooth or silky on the skin. Emollient preparations coat the skin, "pasting down" those pesky scales which are typical of dry skin conditions. Therefore the skin feels smoother (of course!) and softer.

Just for the record, however: Skin dryness (roughness) is not *cured* by emollients. It is merely made to *feel* better.

Emulsions   These are usually one of two types: *oil-in-water*, meaning that droplets of oil have been dispersed in a large amount of water, or *water-in-oil*, meaning, of course, the opposite of oil-in-water.

Most cosmetic emulsions are of the O/W (oil-in-water) type, consisting of about one-quarter oil portion and three-quarters water phase (which includes milk, juices, or other "watery" things). Milk is a typical *natural* O/W emulsion with about 4 percent butterfat (as droplets) dispersed in water.

You yourself have perhaps made a typical W/O emulsion called mayonnaise—by dispersing lemon juice or vinegar (the water phase) into vegetable oil, using egg yolk (lecithin) as the emulsifier. If you are old and wise you may have added a little mustard as an "emulsion stabilizer" (to prevent early separation).

Ethanol (Ethyl Alcohol)   See *Alcohol.*

Extracts   Extracts used as food flavorings are usually alcoholic extracts of the flower, the fruit, the seed or the root of various plants. The plant material is usually shredded first, then soaked in an alcohol-and-water mixture from which the roughage is later filtered off. The "extract" portion is then concentrated by distillation (boiling off, under carefully controlled conditions).

Fennel   A seed herb containing much sulfur, potassium, and organic sodium. Compresses made from fennel tea are soothing to the eyes. Facial packs made from fennel tea and honey have been recommended against wrinkles.

Food Coloring   The "food colors" sold in your local supermarket are not natural products; they are specially approved "certified dyes" (synthetic) which are tightly controlled by the Food and Drug Administration. Every batch made is individually checked for purity and then held in the factory under seal until word is received from Washington that it is approved.

Fuller's Earth   A nonplastic variety of kaolin containing magnesium. Naturally porous; used for filtering and purifying liquids, and in facial packs to remove excessive oiliness. The name derives from its use in "fulling" woolen cloth (shrinking and thickening).

GARLIC This herb has been "known" as an antiseptic for centuries by old wives, but without formal scientific proof. Now it turns out that garlic contains allicin, a compound which Dr. J. H. Bailey found attacks staphylococci, the virulent organisms that cause boils.

Baldness remedies based on garlic juice have been advocated for centuries, usually mixed with bay rum (or alcohol) and olive oil. A recent Russian study used garlic to treat 194 patients with lip and mouth disorders, and reportedly completely healed conditions such as hyperkeratosis and leucoplakia. Simmered in oil for use as an ointment, garlic has been advocated for thousands of years in the Himalayan area (where it originated) for treatment of wounds, pimples, and to arrest tumors (!).

GELATIN The product of partial hydrolysis (cooking, to break down) of animal collagen obtained from skin, bones, sinews, etc. Gelatin—unflavored, without added sugar—is an excellent home source of protein for cosmetic use. Paint it on fingernails to give them strength; put it through your hair (in a shampoo, in a conditioner, or just in water) and you will begin rebuilding damaged hair in a dramatic way, restoring strength and body. Can be bought at most food stores.

GINSENG The famous Chinese herb (it also grows wild in the United States and Canada) which is claimed to be a general tonic, stimulant and life-giver (according to Chinese herbal lore). Its Western name, *Panax quinquefolium*, is related to the Latin *panacea*. Volumes could be written on its history, effects and uses in the East, where it has been employed as a cure-all for thousands of years. Chinese doctors prescribe daily doses of it. Almost the entire American crop is exported—to the Far East, of course!

GLYCERINE A natural humectant, glycerine is the byproduct of soapmaking. (Cooking tallow with lye releases glycerine as the soap forms.) It is sweet-tasting and is most effective when used for chapped lips and hands in preparations such as glycerine and rose-water.

GUM ARABIC Known also as "acacia gum," this is a resinous exudate from acacia trees growing in the Sudan. Huge drops of this resin (called "tears") are picked off the trees and dissolved in water, forming a mucilage used in candy-making, as an emulsion stabilizer in cosmetics, and to fix glazes on ceramics before kiln firing.

HAIR Grows at the rate of about half an inch per month. This simple fact is the saving grace of beauticians, hair chemists, and home experimenters alike; no matter what you do to it, a new crop is always on the way!

Odd Facts Department: The average head has over a hundred thousand hairs, and the life span of each individual hair runs about 180–200 days. That little ball at the end of a plucked hair is *not* the root, so plucking a hair does not result in permanently stopping hair growth in any particular spot.

Humans dyed their hair at least as early as 3000 B.C., when Babylonian women dyed their hair red; women of the Roman Empire favored blond generally, but sometimes they went for blue (during the period just before the birth of Christ, about 30 B.C.).

To make hair grow: Here is a recipe found in an ancient Egyptian pyramid, for the private use of Sest, mother of "the Majesty of the South and the North" (Tety)—"One part paws of a dog, one part kernels of dates, one part hoof of a donkey. Cook thoroughly with oil in an earthen pot and anoint therewith."*

HAIR SPRAYS Nowadays these are all based on synthetic resins of various sorts, generally dissolved in ethanol and pressurized in aerosol cans. But until 1950 or so, many hair sprays were still based largely on shellac, the secretion of the lac insect, which gave a

---

* Denise Nicholas, *Beauty Book* (New York: Simon and Schuster, 1971).

very stiff hairdo (remember "beehive" hairdos?) that was quite difficult to wash out.

HENNA   Is used as a paste which is made from the powdered leaves of a small shrub growing in Egypt and Asia. Henna gives red highlights to the hair, skin or fingernails. Ancient Egyptians thought it indecent *not* to dye their fingernails red, as shown by many mummies found in the Pyramids. Henna was also used by Egyptian ladies to color their breasts and navels, a custom not generally followed in modern times. A nice perfume is also extracted from henna flowers.

HONEY   One of the earliest known humectants. A natural sugar, it is obtained from a "maturing" of nectar, which the bees carry from flowers to their hives. A good hive can put out about twenty pounds of honey per day, which is really fantastic considering that each pound of nectar requires between sixty thousand and eighty thousand trips by individual bees from the flower field to the hive. (Talk about busy bees!)

Honey can clarify soap bars (making them transparent) and help clear shampoos as well.

HUMECTANTS   Materials which hold moisture. They are added to cosmetics for two reasons: to prevent the product itself from drying out (crusting over) when the cap is accidentally left off the jar, and to hold moisture to the skin.

IRISH MOSS   A gum extracted from the red seaweed known as carrageenan. Widely used to make pudding gels, in chocolate milk, and in cosmetics (for hand lotions, wave sets, and clear gels). Buy it at health food stores or drugstores.

KAOLIN   A white clay (sometimes called "china clay") which provides adhesiveness to bath powders and talcum preparations. It also absorbs oils, and reduces facial shine in makeup products. Can be bought at drugstores.

LANOLIN   Wool fat or grease. Makes excellent bases for ointments and creams, due to its extraordinary ability to absorb large amounts of water (and juices, including very acidic juices such as lemon juice). Related to human *Sebum*, lanolin contains appreciable amounts of cholesterol and related materials, which contribute to its moisturizing effect on the skin. Obtainable in drugstores or at some supermarkets.

LAVENDER   A lovely fragrant plant. Teas are occasionally made from the dried flower, but its primary use is for perfume manufacture.

LECITHIN   A phospholipid natural emulsifier found in egg yolk (8 percent of it) and in soybeans. (The Greek word *lekithos* means egg yolk.) Highly emollient on the skin, leaving the skin very smooth. A good spreading agent for cosmetics. Also, an antioxidant for oils, reducing their tendency to go rancid. Sold in health food stores as "liquid lecithin."

LEMON   Highly prized in cosmetics, mostly for its odor. It has been mentioned for centuries as a bleach for freckles. However, the 5 to 8 percent citric-acid content of lemon juice (and its consequent very low pH—*very* acid) make it especially useful in pH lotions, or in "hair-repair treatment" products that help restore bleach-damaged hair or brittle ends.

LICORICE ROOT   When cooked, this produces a black-brown "licorice extract" which is a demulcent in addition to its use as an expectorant and occasionally as a laxative. Licorice extract has been employed as a cure-all for thousands of years, since the days of ancient Egypt and China, and is produced and consumed today at the rate of thousands of tons per year throughout the world. Its active ingredient, glycyrrhetinic acid, is similar to hydrocortisone in its action, reducing inflamations when it is incorporated into skin products.

LYE   An old-fashioned word meaning leaching. (Lye was originally obtained by leaching wood ashes to extract a highly alkaline material called caustic soda, or sodium hydroxide.) Lye is used in soapmaking, reacting with various fats and oils to form soap and glycerine.

Caution: Lye dissolves aluminum and should not be used in aluminum pans. If any spills on the skin, flush with vinegar or lemon juice or other acid (citrus) juices. If any gets in the eye, flush with water for fifteen minutes, then follow with a boric-acid rinse.

MAKEUP REMOVERS   These are either *oily types* (plain mineral oil is generally used for removing mascara from eyelids) or *water-and-alcohol astringent types*, for removing traces of cream.

MARGARINE   "Artificial butter," made (without the help of cows) by emulsifying small amounts of water (or milk) into various vegetable oils (such as corn, peanut, soybean or cottonseed oil), using lecithin as the emulsifier and often deliberately introducing measured amounts of air into the emulsion. If an animal oil (such as tallow) is used, the product is known as oleomargarine. As a cosmetic ingredient, it can be used as a substitute for other fats.

MILK   Used in cosmetics primarily for its protein content, but milk also contributes the emollient properties of its butterfat as well as a significant amount of milk sugar (lactose). Milk has been used directly as a cosmetic lotion.

MINERAL OIL   A mixture of liquid hydrocarbons distilled from petroleum. The cheapest cosmetic ingredient (except for water), it provides slip and sheen. It does not "penetrate" the skin, but tends to stay on the surface. An excellent makeup remover, either as is or in lotions and creams. Can be bought at drugstores or super-markets.

MINK OIL   An oil obtained by careful rendering of the layer of white fat which is found just below the pelt of this very valuable animal. Mink oil has a most unusual type of polyunsaturation which gives it excellent skin-softening properties. This oil is a natural sunscreen and produces excellent sheen on the hair. The feel is not oily; it is velvety smooth, rich, luxurious. Can be purchased by direct mail or in some health food stores.

MOISTURIZERS Substances which hold water to the skin, usually in emulsified form. That way, they help keep it soft and supple. Lanolin products perform this function, as do certain humectants.

NATURAL COLORS See also *Food Coloring*. Natural food colorings are obtainable at health-food stores, and include chlorophyll (blue-green), saffron and annatto (yellow), beet juice (red), caramel (orange-brown), and grape-skin extract (purple). Also available occasionally are henna (orange), logwood (purplish brown), and carbon black or charcoal.

NORMAL SKIN Skin which is fresh, with pores that are hardly visible. "A gift of nature, the dream of many."

OATMEAL A coarse meal consisting primarily of the kernels of shucked oats. Partially cooked oatmeal is sometimes used in soaps intended for teen-age acne problems that need special scrubbing. Also, when impregnated with alcohol and other antiseptics, oatmeal is sometimes used for facial scrubs. For itchy skin conditions, oatmeal is a soothing addition to the bath water.

OILY SKIN This results from overfunctioning sebaceous glands, especially on the face. The condition generally reaches its height during puberty and then gradually decreases. It is typified by a shiny appearance and large pores; alcoholic astringent preparations are recommended for alleviating it.

OINTMENT BASES Used by pharmacists as vehicles for ingredients prescribed by your doctor, ointment bases are interesting take-off points for some cosmetic formulas. The simplest ointment formula is 5 percent each of lanolin and white wax, plus 90 percent petrolatum.

OKRA A vegetable with a long-ribbed pea full of a very special mucilage called gombine (from which we get the word "gumbo," for thickened soups and stews). Gombine is a demulcent emollient material of considerable interest which has been used in making soothing cough syrups and even a "synthetic blood plasma." Gombine can be powdered for long-term storage.

OLIVE OIL Known to the druggist as "sweet oil." It is probably the first oil ever used in cosmetics (going back to the Roman physician Galen—about A.D. 100). Olive oil and (chilled) lime water in approximately equal parts will produce a temporary emulsion which is quite soothing. "Lime water" here refers to slaked lime made from the gardening material, not to lime juice.

PAPAYA A tropical fruit known as the "wonder fruit" due to various healing powers. Contains vitamins A, C, and E, but no starch. Powdered papaya is known as papain, an enzyme tenderizer for tough meat. Seminole Indians applied a fresh papaya leaf to open wounds as a dressing. Papaya is said to guard against halitosis and offensive body odors. Known as *paw paw* in the West Indies, and as *zapote* in Mexico.

PARAFFIN WAX The waxy fraction left over after the kerosene and mineral-oil fractions have been removed from petroleum. You probably know it better as "household wax" for sealing jars of jams and jellies. Paraffin is a mineral wax, in contrast to vegetable waxes you may have met before (carnauba, bayberry, etc.) and animal waxes such as beeswax.

PEACH Nicholas Culpeper said that if the kernels of peaches are bruised and boiled in vinegar and applied to the head, "it marvelously makes the hair to grow again in bald places or where it is too thin." But he wrote that in the early 1600s, and nothing has been heard of the cosmetic powers of the peach since (except for its lovely taste and fragrance!).

PEANUT OIL Sometimes known as "arachis oil." Fairly heavy and slippery, it is similar to olive oil in composition and cosmetic uses.

PECTIN   A mildly acidic gummy material which is extracted from the inner rinds of citrus fruits and apple peels and then powdered. Adding a few apples to other fruits when making jellies helps them to set faster. In cosmetics, pectin is used as an emulsifying aid and for its thickening and gelling properties.

You can extract your own pectin by simmering apple peels in milk or water; strain off all pulpy material after fifteen or twenty minutes, then cook down to a concentrate, which will gel on cooling.

PERFUMES   Can be made from anything that has a strong odor, whether natural or synthetic, whether pleasing or not, whether long-lasting or fleeting. The art of perfumery is to blend all of these bewildering possibilities in ways which are pleasing, which are smooth combinations, which meld with each other to make a "marriage," and, finally, which give approximately the same final fragrance as the initial impression given right out of the bottle. See the chapter on *Natural Perfumes* for more details. Study the formulas in this book; all of them are based on *natural* perfume materials.

Historical notes: King Tutankhamen's tomb when it was opened in 1922, five thousand years or so after he was buried in it, contained ceramic perfume vials which still contained recognizable fragrances! Hieroglyphics on early tombs show that Egyptians knew even then how to "express" citrus rinds, squeezing out perfume oils, and that they operated crude stills as well. The ancient Jews learned these perfuming processes during their exile in Egypt, and after the Exodus they enhanced their own religious ceremonies with myrrh, cinnamon, cassia, and calmus perfume oils, mixed further with animal oils and fats to make ointments which were used at first for the unction of high priests, later for the anointment of kings, and finally for personal adornment by ordinary people.

PEPPERMINT EXTRACT   An alcoholic solution of peppermint oil, which is obtained from the mint plant (*Mentha piperita*). Peppermint oil contains about 28 percent menthol, a cool-tasting and -feeling crystalline material which is also a mild antiseptic. We use peppermint in our cosmetic recipes for this menthol content, which gives a zing to products such as aftershaves.

A small amount of menthol feels cool on the skin and soothes skin suffering from "razor burn" (from too close shaving); however, if two or three times more menthol is used, this effect reverses: now it feels hot and begins to irritate!

PERSIC OIL   See also *Apricot-Kernel Oil*. Peach-kernel oil has also been called "Persic" at times. But for all practical purposes, peach-kernel oil can't be squeezed from peach kernels in commercially useful amounts, so you really can't buy it. Therefore it doesn't exist. Right?

✓ PETROLATUM   Although commonly known as "petroleum jelly," petrolatum is the "in-between fraction" of petroleum—not as heavy as paraffin wax, but not as light as mineral oil.

pH   This is the way chemists refer to the acidity or alkalinity of any product. Neutral pH is 7.0. Anything with a pH under 7 is acid (like lemon juice). A pH over 7 is alkaline (like lye, which is a strong alkali, or soap, which is mildly alkaline).

Normal skin has a pH of 5.5. When it has been "fatigued" by frequent contact with soap or high-pH cosmetics, it can be "restored" by using cosmetics which are in this normal-skin pH range.

PINEAPPLE JUICE   This is quite acid (substitute it only in formulas calling for citrus fruits) and contains bromelain, another of those meat-tenderizing enzymes similar to papain. Has not been explored as much as it should be for cosmetic purposes.

PROTEIN SUBSTANTIVITY   One of those vague phrases which you've perhaps heard in TV commercials or read about in magazine ads. Proteins, of course, are the basic building blocks of all higher life forms (including people). Proteins are big bunches of amino acids glued together in various shapes and in different sequences; chains and spirals of amino acids are really what life is all about.

Recently it was discovered that some proteins stick to other proteins. That stick-to-it-iveness is what we call "substantivity."

Certain proteins, such as those derived from collagen (refined from animal hides and sinews), stick to hair so well that they actually rebuild damaged hair—make it soft and strong again.

QUINCE SEEDS   Come from a rather unpalatable fruit (when raw) which grows in New England, Persia, and many parts of the world. When soaked in water, the seeds release a lovely clear jelly which is demulcent and soothing, and absolutely nontacky—which is the primary quality of interest in cosmetic hand lotions, wave sets, and even colognes. The Portuguese word for "quince," *marmelo*, gives us our word "marmelade," a tart jelly—which is just what cooked quince makes.

ROSE EXTRACT   Actually rose perfume, even though it's sold in some specialty food stores and used in certain recipes of the Mid-East. It has generally been slightly "solubilized" to help it dissolve more easily in foods and drinks. (During World War II there was a fad for rose-perfumed champagne cocktails in London.) More flowers than you think are edible—violets, day-lily buds, and artichokes, for example.

ROSEMARY   A lovely bush with shiny green leaves; an herb of exceptionally fragrant power; an excellent perfume material for home use. It has a wide reputation (among old wives) for stimulating hair growth when used in shampoos or hair rinses.

SAFFLOWER OIL   The richest in unsaturates of all the common vegetable oils, and one of the most difficult to keep from going rancid. Its major constituent is a linoleate triglyceride. In general, unsaturated oils tend to "penetrate" the skin more readily than saturated oils—that is, their slightly greasy feel disappears almost immediately when they are rubbed into the skin.

SAFFRON   A marvelous yellow dye obtained from the flowers of *Colchicum autumnale*. Used for dyeing silk and feathers in ancient times, it was even mentioned in the Biblical Song of Solomon. Its current use is primarily as a food flavoring. Powdered saffron root is astringent.

SEBUM   A fatty material secreted by the sebaceous glands of your skin. Every hair on your head (or anywhere else on your body) has a sebaceous gland attached to its root, which lubricates the hair as it grows out. Sheep sebum is known as lanolin ("wool grease"), and because of its similarity to human sebum it "penetrates" our skin—slips down into those ubiquitous hair shafts, right *through* the skin.

SESAME OIL   A highly unsaturated oil, quite light in texture, and a good natural sunscreen (probably second only to mink oil in this respect). Available in food and health stores.

SHAMPOO   This should really be thought of as a hair beautifier rather than as a hair cleaner. Shampoos generally do not remove all the oil from the hair; otherwise it would become dull and fly-away. The best-selling commercial shampoos have been shown to be those which clean least and, in fact, which sometimes deposit more material than they remove from the hair!

SHORTENING   Cooking fat made from "hydrogenated" oil mixtures, such as palm and soybean oils. Hydrogenation removes all unsaturation, thus transforming the oil into a solid and ensuring that it will no longer go rancid at room temperature.

When buying shortening for cosmetic use, look for the cheapest and simplest one. Check the label! Avoid fancy brands which claim added silicones (to avoid splattering), polyunsaturates, etc. All such additives interfere with your cosmetic requirements, which need a simple saturated triglyceride fat.

SKIN   The "principal outer defense zone of the human body, holding the environment at bay with remarkable success, but only at the expense of continually renewing its outer surface." (Dr. N. J. Van Abbe, 1968.)

SKIN TONE   Its firmness or tightness.

SLIPPERY ELM   The shredded inner bark of the *Ulmus fulva* tree. When soaked or cooked in water, this bark forms a thick *gelée* which is an excellent nutritive food for children and convalescents, or a thickener for cosmetic lotions. The dried inner bark itself, ground to a fine powder, is said to make an excellent poultice for wounds and burns.

SOAP   Technically, soap is any salt of any fatty acid. In practice, however, it is usually made by reacting lye (caustic soda) or caustic potash with beef tallow to which are added small portions of palm oil or coconut oil (see recipe, page 111). Soaps are very alkaline, which sometimes makes them unsuitable for use on tender skin. Soaps are curdled by acid, which is why lemon-juice cosmetics cannot use a soap base. A byproduct of the soapmaking process is *glycerine*.

SOYA, or SOYBEANS   These have twice as much protein (pound for pound) as steak. The oil from soybeans is rich in lecithin and is highly unsaturated. Soybean sprouts can be grown at home in about five days, and are an excellent food.

STARCH   The main reserve carbohydrate of plants, and therefore one of the most widely distributed substances in the vegetable kingdom. Wheat and potato starches were used in powders for changing the color of the hair during the seventeenth and eighteenth centuries. Rice starch was widely used in face powders until fairly recently. Starches absorb moisture, making other powders more free-flowing. See also *Cornstarch* and *Oatmeal*.

STEARIC ACID   A crystalline white waxy material obtainable from almost any natural fat, this is a major ingredient in most bar soaps and many candles, and is present in a large proportion of all cosmetic emulsions made today. Stearic acid gives stiffness to all creams and "pearliness" to some (due to its crystalline nature) and is the emulsifying base (with various amines) of many emulsions.

SUNFLOWER OIL   As you would expect, this is "expressed" from all those sunflower seeds. It is a lovely oil, extraordinarily light in color and texture, ideal for cosmetic uses.

SUNTAN PRODUCTS   If unprotected, skin constantly exposed to the sun ages quickly, becoming shriveled and dried up. This effect is cumulative, and especially pronounced damage is caused by severe sunburning.

Sunscreens are ultraviolet absorbers, materials which hold back part of the harmful ultraviolet radiation of the sun. They work best when they allow just enough of the ultraviolet rays through to produce a slight reddening of the skin, but not any more than that. A few hours later, a deep tan begins to develop, which itself then helps to protect against further damage by the sun's rays.

TALC   A powdered hydrous magnesium silicate, also known as soapstone, or steatite. A natural ore (the softest of all "rocks"), it is dug out of the ground, powdered and washed. Talc occurs in "platelet" form; flat flakes rather than sharp crystals, these platelets slide over each other as you touch them, giving that incredibly rich soft-smooth feel of talcum powder.

TANNIC ACID   An astringent substance found in the bark and fruit of many plants, such as oak barks, nutgalls, and various tea leaves. It is a burn remedy and is quite soothing to irritated skin in general.

TAPIOCA   A granular farina-like food extracted from cassava starch by drying it while moist, on heated plates. The word itself is of Brazilian origin. Tapioca is used to thicken various products, and as a nutritious pudding dessert.

TARRAGON   An herb used for culinary purposes, and also in perfumery and liqueurs. The dried leaves (sometimes sold under the European name, *estragon*) can be soaked in alcohol to extract a greenish perfume oil of considerable interest in cosmetics.

TEAS The choicest tea leaves are harvested at altitudes above four thousand feet and are named (like wines) after various districts in which they grow (Darjeeling, Assam, etc.). The leaves are dried in the sun. The oolong varieties are partially fermented before drying; they are more astringent than black teas, but less astringent than green teas. Cosmetic uses for teas depend on their astringency and on their (related) tannic-acid content (for sun-screening effects).

TINCTURE An alcoholic solution.

UNSATURATED OILS Without even attempting to explain a very complicated part of organic chemistry, it should be noted that unsaturated oils (*"poly*unsaturation" refers to unsaturation in several locations of the oil molecule) generally tend to disappear quickly when rubbed into the skin. This quality is useful in formulating cosmetics, as the unsaturated oil gives a lighter skin feel and seems to "penetrate"—although this is not always literally true. Other oils (saturated or hydrogenated oils) stay on the surface more and therefore feel much more greasy.

VINEGAR From the French *vin aigre* ("sour wine"). Basically, dilute acetic acid obtained from the fermentation of wines, cider or rice; occasionally it is flavored with additives such as tarragon.

WATER Although quite satisfactory for drinking, water may not be suitable for cosmetics if it has too high a mineral content. Emulsions are affected by hard water and the presence of chlorine, which also cannot be tolerated. If you know that you live in a hard-water area, and are having trouble with your cosmetic emulsions, switch to "softened" or distilled water and try again. Microorganisms (which may multiply later in the closed jars or bottles) are the biggest problem with "potable" water, as they are in ordinary milk. (Food-grade milk usually contains more bacteria than are allowed by law in cosmetics!)

WHEAT-GERM OIL A major source of vitamins A and E. Grain-germ oils in general are interesting for cosmetics, due to their high vitamin and phytoestrogen contents. Wheat-germ oil contains 80 percent unsaturated fatty acids.

WITCH HAZEL   More properly, *Extract* of witch hazel, distilled from twigs of the spotted alder bush which grows in New England. The bark and leaves of this plant are astringent, and the fluid extract (containing 14 percent alcohol, like a good wine) is soothing to skin irritated by insect bites, sunburn, shaving, etc. Witch hazel's astringency is presumably due to the presence of *tannins*.

YOGURT   Fermented whole milk, produced commercially by evaporating milk to about half its volume, maintaining the temperature at about 120° F for twelve hours. "Maya" (a "starter culture obtained from previous batches of yogurt) is added to start this fermentation process. Has some antibacterial properties.

ZINC OXIDE   A creamy white pigment which is mildly antiseptic and soothing. Use only USP grade (from the drugstore) for cosmetics! "Technical grades" used in paints and ceramics may contain lead or arsenic.